Arthur Hadrian Allcroft

Outlines of Roman History from 133 to 27 B.C

Arthur Hadrian Allcroft

Outlines of Roman History from 133 to 27 B.C

ISBN/EAN: 9783337044725

Printed in Europe, USA, Canada, Australia, Japan

Cover: Foto ©ninafisch / pixelio.de

More available books at **www.hansebooks.com**

The University Tutorial Series.

OUTLINES OF
ROMAN HISTORY
FROM 133 TO 27 B.C.

BY

A. H. ALLCROFT, M.A. Oxon.,

FIRST-CLASS HONOURMAN AT MODERATIONS AND AT FINAL CLASSICAL EXAM.,
AUTHOR OF 'ROME UNDER THE OLIGARCHS,' 'THE EARLY PRINCIPATE,' ETC.,

AND

W. F. MASOM, M.A. Lond.,

FIRST-CLASS HONOURMAN IN CLASSICS, UNIVERSITY EXHIBITIONER, FIRST-CLASS
IN CLASSICAL TRIPOS, CAMBRIDGE; EDITOR OF LIVY III., V., TACITUS,
ANNALS I., II., HERODOTUS VI.

REPRINTED FROM 'THE TUTORIAL HISTORY OF ROME.'

LONDON   W. B. CLIVE,
13 BOOKSELLERS ROW, STRAND, W.C.

INTRODUCTORY CHAPTER.

§ 195. Growth of Roman power.—§ 196. Effects of the Hannibalic War: Social Changes.—§ 197. Political changes: the Senatorial Monopoly of Power.—§ 198. Condition of the Subject Italians.—§§ 199, 200. The Provinces: their Condition and Organization.—§ 201. The Equestrian Order.—§ 202. Summary.

§ 195. WITH the year 133 B.C. commences the history of those successive revolutions which, originating in the attempt to restore a proper balance between the parties of the senate and of the people, ultimately gave over both to the absolute authority of one man.

Rome had long been an imperial city. During two and a half centuries she had extended her power successively over the Sabines and Latins at her gates, over Campania and the Samnites, over the Etruscans and the Gauls of Northern Italy, until at length in 270 B.C. she was mistress of an undivided Italy. Her peninsular dominion was rounded off by the acquisition of Sicily, Sardinia, and Corsica, after the First Punic War (264—241 B.C.). Then came the terrible struggle with Hannibal (218—202 B.C.). That crisis passed, she set out upon a career of foreign conquest, which gave her new dominions

Dominion of Rome, 133 B.C.

in Greece, in Africa, and in Asia,[1] and made her the acknowledged head of the Mediterranean powers.

§ 196. Hannibal had failed to accomplish his oath in his lifetime, but his curse was fulfilled in the legacy of revolution which he left behind him. For there followed two prime results from his invasion of Italy : socially the whole breadth of Italy was changed, and politically the sovereignty of Rome was transferred from the people to the senate.

Social Changes.

The war with Hannibal desolated the farms of Italy, and killed off thousands of her yeomen. Those who survived were more familiar with war than with industrial pursuits. Many of these had neither the means to replace lost stock and implements, nor to subsist until their farms could again be made productive.

Decay of Agriculture.

They therefore abandoned husbandry, and either sought a livelihood as professional soldiers, or drifted to the towns as the clients of wealthier men. There commenced a "Rural Exodus." Labour became scarce, and slaves were imported to supply the demand; but as slave-labour, being unskilled and unwilling, could not be profitably employed in raising crops, particularly in the face of the active competition of the more productive corn-lands of Africa and Sicily, the land was largely laid down in grass. Grass-farming needs no labour beyond that of a few cattlemen, an occupation for which a slave is well enough fitted. Its profits moreover increase with the increase of acreage. Hence free labour ceased to be in demand, and freeholds of only moderate size tended to be swallowed up in the new

---

[1] Her provinces at this date were as follows :—Sicilia (constituted 241 B.C.), Sardinia with Corsica (227 B.C.), Hispania Citerior and Ulterior (197 B.C.), Macedonia with Achaea (148 B.C.), and Africa (146 B.C.). The province of Asia was constituted in the year with which this period commences, 133 B.C. (See the map, p. 350.)

and **enormous** cattle-runs (*latifundia*) **of the wealthy.**
There was no longer need or room for the few who might have wished to continue the old way of life. They were bought out, starved out, or even wrongfully evicted, by such as could afford to purchase slaves and stock **large** ranches; **so** that whole districts were depopulated, **and** the towns became congested by the influx of men of no property and no occupation, **who must** subsist **either by dishonest means or by attaching themselves to the wealthy.** Hence on the one hand came **crime, and on** the other servility, **itself** the first step to crime, immorality, **and the loss of patriotism.** For seventy years this **process went on,** until at the present date Rome was a city in which some 2000 persons held the monopoly of wealth, **while there was a** countless rabble of dependent paupers,[1] slowly starving into desperation. **There** was indeed scattered throughout Italy, **as** also in the transmarine provinces, a large extent of Public **Land,** *i.e.* such portion of the conquered territories as had been neither freely restored **to its** original occupants, nor sold for the **benefit of the Treasury,** nor distributed in the form of allotments amongst needy citizens. **For the most part** such **land was of** second-rate quality, fitted for little beside pasturage, and **in** theory it was let **to** such as cared to take it on payment of a fixed rental (*scriptura*) for every head of stock turned out upon it. But from the **very** earliest times **of** Rome's conquests the theory had been forgotten: the public land had fallen into the hands first of the patricians and subsequently of

<small>Decline of Population.</small>

<small>And of Morality.</small>

<small>The Ager Publicus.</small>

---

[1] It must be remembered that there was no free artisan class to counterbalance the decay of the yeomen. The Roman *civis*, however poor, despised manual labour; and if he had desired to undertake it, he could **not hope** to compete with the more skilled labour of cheap slaves.

their successors the wealthy class—the class which least needed it. By the Licinio-Sextian Rogations (367 B.C.) an attempt had been made to remedy this abuse, the articles of that Act providing that—

(*a*) No citizen was to occupy more than 500 acres of public land, or to keep more than 100 oxen and 500 sheep on the public pasture.

(*b*) A landlord was to employ a number of free labourers proportioned to that of his slaves employed in agriculture;

but the old state of things speedily recurred, and the officers of the Treasury, while conniving at the illegalities whereby their wealthy partisans obtained possession of the bulk of the land, suffered them also to evade payment of the lawful rent. The land was monopolized by the few, and as time went on it became to all intents and purposes the private property of the occupants, to be alienated or bequeathed at their pleasure. At the present date it was in many cases impossible to say what was, and what was not, *ager publicus*. Thus much only was certain, that neither the Treasury nor the mass of the population derived any benefit from it, but that its profits accrued entirely to a limited number of wealthy men, mostly indeed Romans, but including also not a few Italians.

§ 197. As with things social, so also with things political: political power, in theory the prerogative of Roman citizens at large, was restricted in effect to a clique of some 300 or 400 families in Rome. These represented the national wealth, and from these were elected alike the senate and the magistrates.[1] In theory of course all magistracies

Political Changes.

Rome a Plutocracy.

---

[1] The roll of magistrates at this date is as follows: two consuls who took the command abroad or presided in the senate at home; six praetors, of whom two (the *praetor urbanus* and *praetor peregrinus*) acted as the chief legal authorities in the capital, while four more were sent out every year to administer some of the newly-formed provinces —Sicily, Sardinia and Corsica, the two Spains, &c.; two censors for

were still elective, and at the absolute disposal of the people assembled in the centuries or the tribes; but in fact the votes of the people were at the command of the wealthy few, for the starving voter will sell his suffrage to him who offers the highest price. The rich therefore studied to reduce their poorer fellow-citizens to a state of impotence, merely keeping them alive by doles of food, and humouring them with games and shows. To the rich fell the offices of consul, censor, praetor, and aedile, even of quaestor and tribune, with their various prerogatives of military command and provincial governorship, of judicial authority and of legislative initiative, and of finance. From the number of those who had enjoyed these offices the censor filled up vacancies in the senate, which in its turn directed and controlled the election of new officers. The powers and privileges of government were in fact syndicated by the rich. The mass of the citizens was powerless, hopeless, disorganized. The Senatorial Monopoly of Office.

The usurpation of power by the senate had been inevitable, if unjust, for the tribes and centuries were no longer fit to govern. The qualified voters were too widely scattered over Italy, too little experienced, and too little educated, to take an intelligent part in questions of policy and administration which did not directly affect themselves; and while possessing no organization which might enable them to assert themselves even in questions of more immediate concern, they were compelled by want Incapacity of the Comitia.

---

finance and the revision of the census lists; four aediles (two curule and two plebeian) for police; eight quaestors, of whom two (*quaestores urbani*) supervised the revenue at Rome, two (*quaestores militares*) accompanied the army as paymasters to the troops, while four (*quaestores classici*) were stationed in different parts of the peninsula to collect such sums as the subjugated Italians paid to Rome. Ten tribunes were annually elected, but the dictatorship had been shelved since the fiasco of Fabius and Minucius (217 B.C.).

to use their votes mostly as a means of livelihood. On the other hand, effective government demands the attention of a limited number of experienced men. So the senate became increasingly powerful, while the Comitia fell practically into desuetude: the Centuries met merely to go through the form of electing consuls, censors, and praetors, or of giving their sanction to a declaration of war[1]; the Tribes met only to ratify bills sent down to them by the senate. To the senate, and its nominees the magistrates, was left every function of government, the conduct of war, the making of peace, the control of domestic and foreign policy, of finance and religion, of the subject Italians and of the provinces; while even the jealously guarded power of capital punishment was occasionally usurped by the senate's Ultimate Decree. Rarely did any but a member of the governing clique rise even to the humblest magistracy. Those who had once held a curule office became thereby members of the privileged class, the *Optimates*, entitled to demand similar dignities for their descendants; but he who by chance crept into office, like Cato, with no recommendation of birth or wealth, and on the strength of personal merit alone, was despised as a *novus homo*—an upstart of no ancestry. On the other hand, there were certain enactments

Margin note: Extension of Powers of Senate.

---

[1] By a change which must have been effected after 241 B.C., when the last of the thirty-five tribes was created, the Comitia Centuriata was to some extent assimilated to the Comitia Tributa. There is no certainty as to the details, but the following explanation may be accepted as probable: it was organized on the basis of the tribes, the citizens in the thirty-five tribes being divided into five classes, each ranked as in the Servian constitution according to property; and each of these five classes comprised one century of *seniores* and one century of *iuniores*. Thus the reformed Comitia Centuriata would consist of three hundred and fifty centuries, of which seventy belonged to each of the five propertied classes. In addition the eighteen equestrian centuries continued to exist, but their precedence in voting was abolished.

designed to prevent any one member of the ruling class from obtaining too large a share of the profits and privileges of government, as for instance the *Lex Villia Annalis* of 180 B.C., which decreed (1) that no citizen was eligible to office unless he had served ten campaigns; (2) that election to the offices of quaestor, praetor, and consul must be successive (*i.e.* that election to the consulship was not valid unless the quaestorship and praetorship had been previously held); (3) that two clear years must elapse between the tenure of one office and the next. From this it followed, since no Roman could serve until at least seventeen years of age, that he could not be quaestor until twenty-eight, praetor until thirty-one, or consul until thirty-four.[1]

The Lex Annalis.

§ **198.** The subject Italians themselves were not more content than the mass of the citizens. The various communities which made up Italy were (1) citizen-colonists, (2) passive citizens (*cives sine suffragio*), (3) Latins, and (4) allies (*socii*).[2] After the second **Punic**

The Latins and allies.

---

[1] In Cicero's time a man could not be quaestor until he was thirty, praetor until forty, or consul until forty-three.

[2] Instances of these various ranks are the following:

(1) Citizen colonies. These were mostly on the sea coast. The earliest was Ostia, of which the foundation is ascribed to the regal period. Others were Antium (338 B.C.), Tarracina (329), Puteoli (founded with seven others in 194). The inhabitants of these places had all the rights (public and private) of Roman citizens.

(2) Communities of passive citizens. Such were Capua, Cumae and Atella in Campania, the Volscian Privernum and Arpinum, the Samnite Allifae. The inhabitants of these possessed at first only the private rights (*commercium* and *conubium*) of the citizen, but gradually such communities were (like Arpinum) raised to full citizen rank.

(3) Latin colonies. To this category belonged the inland fortresses established by Rome to ensure the subjection of Italy. Among them may be named Luceria (314), Narnia (299), Ariminum (268), Beneventum (268), Brundusium (244), Cremona and Placentia (218).

(4) Allies. Such were Tibur and Praeneste in Latium, Neapolis in Campania, and the Greek cities of the southern coast. In the same

war the Romans endeavoured to widen the gap between citizens and non-citizens, for although those communities which possessed the passive franchise (*civitas sine suffragio*) were advanced to the position of full citizen-towns, the Latins were humiliated until they had practically no rights at all. Originally the *ius Latii* had specially ensured the right of any one possessing it to migrate to Rome at pleasure; but in the case of all Latin colonies founded after 268 B.C. a Latin could only settle in the capital provided he had filled a magistracy in his native town. Such Latins as tried to secure illegally a domicile in Rome, were on occasion summarily expelled and dismissed to their native towns. After the foundation of Aquileia in 184 B.C. no further Latin colonies were planted in Italy. The result of all this was that the entire peninsula parted into two hostile camps, that of the Roman citizens and that of the non-citizens.

The grievances of the Italians[1] were many and various. In time of war they were called upon to provide as many foot-soldiers and far more horse than the Romans. In spite of this they were not treated on equal terms with the citizens when land and booty was distributed. Generally they enjoyed the right of self-government, but it was always possible for this to be overridden by a law passed at Rome or even by a simple decree of the senate. While the Roman citizen was secure from capital or corporal punishment, an Italian, even though he had filled the highest

Grievances of the Italians.

---

group came the Samnites, Lucanians, &c., but their position differed materially according to the terms they had made when submitting to Roman authority.

[1] In 133 B.C. the name *Italia* denoted only that part of the peninsula which lay to the south of the Macra and the Aesis. In the time of Caesar the boundaries were the Macra and the Rubicon. *Italia* did not extend to the Alps until the reign of Augustus.

offices in his native town, might be scourged, beheaded, and generally maltreated at the caprice of any Roman official. Yet the Italians were in many respects satisfied with Roman rule, and before deciding their claims by an appeal to arms tried repeatedly to acquire the franchise by peaceful means. The delay was partly due to the fact that in most of the Italian communities the upper and lower classes were opposed to each other. The wealthy Italians had been allowed to share in the public land of Rome, and so did not resent so keenly as the poorer classes the unjust pressure of military service and the unfair division of spoil. On the other hand, they eagerly desired the *ius honorum*, so that they might be admitted to the ranks of the aristocracy that was now ruling the world.

§ 199. The provincials again had their own particular grievances. The *provincia* [1] of a magistrate meant primarily the sphere in which his powers as such were exercised; hence its use to represent any part of the Roman empire which was habitually committed to the control of a governor. By the laws of ancient warfare everything which belonged to a conquered people passed by conquest into the hands of their victors. Theoretically then, the entire area of a province belonged to the Romans; in practice only a small portion was taken over as public domain to be leased to new occupants for the benefit of the state. By far the larger portion was left in the hands of its original possessors as tenants who paid to the state a certain rental (*stipendium*), usually equivalent to one-tenth of the annual income from such lands. Commonly such rental was taken in money, and was therefore a definite annual tax (*capitatio* and *tributum soli*); in the case of Sicily it was

Taxes.

---

[1] The word is probably a contraction of *pro-videntia*, "something put in one's charge."

levied in kind (*decumae*). Such of the inhabitants as possessed no land were subject to a poll-tax (*capitatio*); and all were liable to custom-duties (*vectigalia*) according to a regular scale on products such as metals, marble and salt.

As in Italy, the communities were of several ranks.

<small>Various Classes of Towns.</small>
(1) *Coloniae.*—These were miniature Romes sent out into the provinces to form strategic positions whence Roman forces and Roman civilization could be brought to bear on the province. (Transmarine colonization only dates from the time of C. Gracchus, 123 B.C.)

(2) *Coloniae Latinae.*—These were such towns as possessed the rights of Latin citizens. The first extension of these rights to entire communities of provincials occurred in the case of Transpadane Gaul (§ 235).

(3) *Civitates Foederatae.*—Cities such as had by their loyalty to Rome earned a definite *foedus* securing to them the exercise of their own laws and jurisdiction, and making them liable to the governor's interference only in cases of life and death affecting a Roman *civis*. They enjoyed almost complete independence in home affairs, but were bound to have no foreign policy save that dictated by Rome.

(4) *Civitates Liberae et Immunes.*—A small class of towns or states which, though not possessing the guarantee of a special *foedus*, yet enjoyed a position virtually equal to that of the foregoing. They were exempt from taxation and impost in any shape, and remained entirely independent in name at least.

(5) *Civitates Stipendiariae.*[1]—The mass of the provincial communities, non-privileged towns which paid tribute to Rome.

The policy of Rome was to let the subject peoples govern themselves in the main, and thereby to save the cost of maintaining a large staff of officials amongst them. One governor and half-a-dozen minor officers sufficed for a kingdom. In return Rome took only a sum—often smaller than that which they had paid to their own monarchs when free—sufficient to defray the cost of defending them,

---

[1] In illustration, the case of Sicily may be cited, where communities belonging to each of the last three classes are found. Messana is an instance of the *civitas foederata*. Next to this favoured city were five *civitates liberae et immunes*, Centuripa, Alesa, Panormus, Segesta, and Halicyae. The rest, and the great majority, were *civitates stipendiariae*. There were neither Latin nor citizen colonies in Sicily.

which duty now of course fell upon Rome. They were not asked to find troops for the Roman service, and they were allowed to practise their own religion and customs. In point of fact, Roman manners and customs rapidly spread abroad. Few nations made any great resistance to the process of imperceptible Romanization, which was indeed favoured by the wealthier provincials, who delighted to ape the style and manners of their rulers, the aristocracy of Rome. *General Policy of Rome.*

§ 200. To each province was sent a governor, either consular or praetorian, to maintain the influence of Rome, to defend the country from foreign attack, to watch over the conduct and policy of the people, and to decide, or remit to Rome for decision, judicial cases involving loss of life or other serious points. His year of office embraced a series of assizes held at regular centres (*conventus*) of his own choosing, whereat he settled any suits referred to his arbitration. He had an allowance from the state for his travelling expenses, and the provincials were ordered by the senate to provide him with certain necessaries, such as corn, salt, etc., at a rate fixed beforehand. Beyond this he had theoretically no claims upon his province. In practice he could find means enough to enrich himself at the expense of the people, and hence arose the terrible fact that a provincial administration might be made the royal road to wealth. The governor could not leave his province until his successor arrived, nor delay his departure after that event. *The Governor.*

He was assisted by a number of *legati* of his own choosing, proportionate to the extent of his province. Their duty was to aid him with their counsel in peace and war, and to divide with him the labour of administering justice. *The Legati.*

His only other assistant was the quaestor, whose duties were solely financial, though in case of need he might be called upon to command in the field and to assist at the tribunals. He was charged with the superintendence of the tax-collections, the payment of the governor and his *legati*, and in some degree with everything which concerned the finances of the provinces.

<small>The Quaestor.</small>

The governor was in fact a monarch. His power was virtually absolute while it lasted, for the senate was far away and was content if no serious abuses came to its notice. There was every temptation for an unscrupulous and needy governor to rob his subjects, while they had no redress but to appeal to the senate. Now the governor was himself almost always one of the senatorial oligarchy, and was therefore sure of as much protection as the senate could decently accord. If he were impeached, he must be tried before a senatorial court, where judge and jury had every reason to acquit him if possible, for each of them expected in his turn to be a governor and to receive the same indulgence. Nevertheless, good governors were not altogether wanting; and the provincials at least enjoyed peace and security. They had some protection, too, in the fact that many of them became the clients of leading Roman nobles who were in duty bound to aid them in every possible way: so the Marcelli were the *patroni* of Sicily, Gracchus was the *patronus* of many Spanish towns. Complaints against the governors commenced at an early date, and in 149 B.C. was established by the *Lex Calpurnia* a standing court, composed of senators, to hear prosecutions *de Repetundis*, that is, for extortion. This was the earliest of those standing commissions (*quaestiones perpetuae*) which became of importance after the time of

<small>Position of the Governor.</small>

<small>Lex Calpurnia de Repetundis, 149 B.C.</small>

C. Gracchus, 122 B.C., as the subject of perpetual quarrels between the senate and the Equestrian Order.

§ **201.** With the growth of the provinces is intimately connected the rise of the Equestrian Order (*ordo equester*) or knights (*equites*), a class which in some sort formed a link between the senate and the lower orders. By this time (133 B.C.) the term Equites had come to mean not only the state cavalry, but also, with the exception of senators, all who were sufficiently wealthy to possess the property required for a member of the eighteen centuries of horse, that is, 400,000 sesterces. The eighteen centuries of horse existed now only as so many votes in the comitia; they were no longer called upon for service in the field, and they only appeared in full armour once a year, when on the Ides of July they rode in procession in honour of the victory of Lake Regillus. As senators had by a *Lex Claudia* of 218 B.C. been forbidden to engage in trade, the whole of the financial operations of the state fell to these capitalists. The knights formed themselves into great companies, which undertook the farming of the revenues as a speculation. In this capacity they received the name of *publicani*. They paid a stated sum annually into the treasury, and in return recouped themselves from the provincials. The actual collection lay with their agents, the tax-collectors; and just as it was to the interest of the Equites to get as much as possible out of their agents, so the latter in turn used every possible means to extort money from the subject peoples (*stipendiarii*). Collector, capitalist, and governor alike combined to enrich themselves at the expense of the provinces. The Equites protected their agents, and were themselves protected by the fact that they were themselves men of wealth like the senators, and too valuable as political allies in the

The Equestrian Order.

comitia to be lightly offended. The quarrel between the two orders did not break out until C. Gracchus initiated his reforms.

§ 202. There were then materials enough for revolution. Within Rome, an entire population, to speak roughly, was living on charity, without the ability to remedy their position by constitutional means in the face of the well-organized power of the combined Senatorial and Equestrian Orders, forced to live in the idleness which most encourages agitation. Without the walls, the mass of the subject Italians were at length finding courage to propound their claim to some share in the advantages of a government of which they had been the involuntary creators, and were still the best supporters. On all hands there was beggary, starvation, and lawlessness; fertile lands reverting to desolation, towns dwindling, and villages disappearing, a free populace making way for a population of slaves recruited by thousands from every race of the Mediterranean. Justice was non-existent, remedial measures unthought-of. The Roman world was at peace indeed, but it was such a peace as in France preceded the Great Revolution. It was infinitely to the credit of the Romans and of the Italians that they had endured patiently for so long a time, and that they struggled for half a century more to obtain redress by less violent means before they finally made the appeal to arms.

CHAPTER IX.

THE COMMENCEMENT OF THE REVOLUTION.

§§ 203—205. Tiberius Gracchus.—§ 206. The Province of Asia.—§§ 207—214. **Gaius Gracchus** and his Legislation.—§ 215. The Province of Gallia Narbonensis.—§§ 216—220. The Jugurthine War.—§§ 221—225. War against the German **Tribes.**—§ 226. Sicilian Slave Wars.—§§ 227—231. Events at Rome: **Saturninus** to Drusus.—§§ 232—235. The Social War.—§§ 236—240. Sulla, Marius and Cinna.—§§ 241—246. The First and Second Mithradatic Wars.—§§ 247—254. Sulla's Return and Legislation.

§ **203**. That Tib. **Sempronius Gracchus who had** pacified Spain, 179 B.C., left in the charge of his wife Cornelia two sons; the elder, now about **thirty** years of age and tribune of the people (133 B.C.), was **Tiberius,** the younger **was Gaius.** The elder son had distinguished himself **by personal bravery at the siege of Carthage,** and had seen service in **the army of Spain,** where his word had saved the army of Mancinus from destruction, 137 B.C. He was brother-in-law of Scipio Aemilianus, for his sister was married to that great general; and he himself had wedded the daughter of App. Claudius Pulcher, a leading noble, consular and ex-censor. While on his journeys to and from **Spain** he had marked the desolation of Etruria; he now came forward to propose a remedy.

The first attack on the Senate.

His ideas of reform **were** not altogether new. C. Laelius, the close friend **of** Aemilianus, had only abandoned similar ideas because he foresaw that revolution would ensue—moderation which earned him the

Proposals of Tib. Gracchus.

name of Sapiens, "the Prudent." Since the Licinian Rogations (367 B.C.) nothing had been done to prevent the occupation of the state lands by the wealthy: and though those Rogations were still unrepealed, nobody dreamt of enforcing them, and they were now a dead letter. The depopulation of Italy, which threatened to leave Rome without the materials for an army while it filled her streets with beggars, was due to the misappropriation of the public lands and the spread of slave-labour: therefore after taking counsel with App. Claudius, P. Licinius Crassus Mucianus the Chief Pontiff, and P. Mucius Scaevola the best lawyer in Rome and consul for the year, Tiberius brought before the comitia the following proposals, amounting to a re-enactment of the Licinian Laws:—

(a) That no person should occupy more than 500 *iugera* of public land, with 250 extra for each son: the total amount so occupied by one family not to exceed 1000 *iugera*.
(b) That all land thus recovered should be distributed at a small rent to the poor (Italians as well as Romans) in lots of 30 *iugera*, inalienable and hereditary.
(c) That a certain proportion of free labourers should be employed on all estates.
(d) That the redistribution of land should be managed by a standing commission of three, specially appointed and maintained by the state.

§ **204.** The bill attacked the entire wealthy class of Rome and of Italy, just as it offered relief to the whole of the pauper population; for in the colonies, municipia, and allied communities alike, the rich had both seized on the public land and ousted the small farmers from their holdings. All the rich were therefore in arms against the measure. Tiberius did not lay his proposals before the senate, as was customary, but referred the matter directly to the tribes. The country tribes were enthusiastic in their support, and flocked to Rome in immense numbers to vote for the bill.

The Land Commission.

On the day of voting a fellow-tribune, M. Octavius, vetoed the bill. No vote could be taken: Tiberius retaliated by using his powers of veto against every act of the magistrates, until the tribes were summoned anew. The bill was vetoed a second time by Octavius. Then Tiberius did an unconstitutional thing; he summoned the tribes again, and put to them the question whether they would depose Octavius. They decided in the affirmative, and Octavius was dragged from the tribunes' bench. Then the bill was again put and carried, and as commissioners to execute it were appointed Tiberius himself, his brother Gaius, and his father-in-law App. Claudius.

The senate was beaten, but for the moment contented itself with obstruction. Tiberius' term of office would expire soon (Dec. 10th, 133 B.C.), when it could impeach him; for he could not, in strict law, be re-elected for the ensuing year. Meantime it voted the commissioners no adequate supplies, and watched the difficulties which beset them. There were no means of determining what lands were public and what were not. Everywhere there were endless disputes. Those against whom judgment went, very many of them wealthy Italian *socii*, swelled the ranks of the opposition. Nevertheless the allotments began.

§ **205.** Tiberius felt that he was falling, and made new bids for popular support. Just at this time died Attalus III., the last king of Pergamus, bequeathing all his belongings to the Roman state. Tiberius gave notice of a bill to devote the funds so acquired to providing the new settlers with stock for their farms. Next he talked of extending the franchise to all Italians, of shortening the period of military service, of weakening the power of the senate in the jury-courts by extending the right of service to the equestrian order.

Fall of Tiberius.

In this way he hoped to win his re-election as tribune for 132 B.C. As tribune he would at least be safe from impeachment, whereas now he was not secure even against assassination. The senate determined to prevent his re-election. On the day of voting the tribes began to poll for him; but the senatorial party declared that his re-election was illegal, and nothing was done. On the morrow both parties were prepared to use force, and P. Scipio Nasica, a bitter opponent of Gracchus, called upon the consul to save the state. When the consul Scaevola refused to shed a citizen's blood, Nasica cried out that the state was deserted by its guardians: he would defend it himself. He led the way to the brow of the Capitol where Tiberius was standing with 3000 of his followers, fell upon them suddenly and put them to flight. Tiberius stumbled as he endeavoured to escape and was struck down by one of the tribunes. Three hundred of his partisans fell, while many more were afterwards put to death by a special commission of the senate.

§ **206**. The death of Attalus III. occurred when the senate was too busy to attend to foreign affairs, and while it tarried, Aristonicus, a natural son of Attalus II., appeared as a claimant for the throne. During the year 132 B.C. he was defeated off Cyme by an Ephesian fleet, but in the following year, having called to arms the slaves, he made himself master of Samos and much of the adjoining seaboard. The senate now determined to send an armed force to Asia. Both consuls were eager for the command. P. Licinius Crassus Mucianus, who was also Chief Pontiff, after forbidding his colleague Flaccus, the Flamen Dialis, to leave Rome, secured the prize for himself by a vote of the people; but his selfish-

Acquisition of Pergamus.

ness cost him dear, for he was defeated and killed by Aristonicus in 131 B.C. His successor, the consul M. Perpenna, avenged the defeat, blockaded the pretender in Stratonicea, a Carian town, and forced him to surrender (130 B.C.). The kingdom of Pergamus was then settled by M'. Aquillius, consul for 129 B.C., assisted by a commission of ten senators. Now was constituted the province of Asia, embracing Mysia, Lydia, and the major part of Caria. The southern portion of Caria was given to the Rhodians, and Phrygia went to the king of Pontus, Mithradates V., who had sent troops to assist the Romans; but in 120 B.C. the latter country was taken back and added to Asia, which was, and always remained, the richest of the provinces.

The Province of Asia, 129 B.C.

§ **207.** Although Tiberius was dead, his work had not been in vain. **His** place as Land Commissioner was taken by **P.** Licinius Crassus Mucianus, who, as above related, fell in Asia, 131 B.C., and about the same time died another Commissioner, App. Claudius. The vacancies were filled by Carbo the tribune and M. Fulvius Flaccus, both leaders of the popular party, and the allotments continued. **The work was** real, for within the next decade **the** census showed an increase of 70,000 citizens, most **of** whom must have owed their **status to** the new law. About 129 B.C. the wealthy Latins **and Italians**, with whose tenure the commission was now interfering, broke out into protest, and declared that their property was being confiscated. **The** poorer members **of** the Italian community on the other hand were eager that the laws should be enforced. Both parties appeared in Rome, and called on Scipio Aemilianus, the most powerful of the citizens, to decide between them. Scipio, who had since his

The Italians and the Land Commission.

return from Numantia become more and more identified with the aristocrats, declared in favour of the wealthy Italians; and by this attitude, though heretofore a favourite of the people, he now forfeited their affection. But any collision was averted by his death. One day after making a great speech in the senate he was found dead in bed. Later generations accused Carbo of murdering him, but there seems no valid ground for supposing that he met with foul play. So perished the conqueror of Carthage and Numantia, aged 56, in the winter of 129 B.C. Nevertheless he had virtually ended the work of the commission, for he had secured a decree of the people transferring its duties to the consul for the year, C. Sempronius Tuditanus; and as the latter quitted Rome to conduct a campaign against the Iapydes, a piratical tribe of Illyricum, the agrarian distributions came to an end.

Death of Scipio Aemilianus, 129 B.C.

§ 208. The bitterness which had for generations prevailed between Italians and Romans became now a new element of political discord, for the former began to demand the franchise. The Romans, the poor almost as much as the wealthy, were jealous of their own special privileges and resolved to keep them; and when the question was raised, a tribune carried a motion for expelling all non-Romans from the city, 126 B.C. Thereupon M. Fulvius Flaccus in his consulate, 125 B.C., retorted, by proposing

The Italians demand the Franchise.

That any Latin or Italian ally should be allowed to ask for the Roman citizenship, and to get a vote of the comitia on his request.

Flaccus met with little support even from the party he professed to lead. Carbo had already gone over to the senate, and C. Gracchus was absent in Sardinia. The proposal was defeated, and its author removed by being despatched into Gaul to carry on war against the Salluvii.

Instantly the town of Fregellae, one of the most important of the Latin colonies, rose in arms to obtain satisfaction by force, 125 B.C. Fortunately for Rome there was dissension among the insurgents themselves, and Fregellae was betrayed, rased to the ground, and its place taken by a new citizen-colony at Fabrateria. *Revolt of Fregellae, 125 B.C.* So speedy and decisive a punishment checked whatever disaffection there was. For a space the question of enfranchising the Italians slept, but a fresh and formidable agitator was now on the scene, one who for a few months was virtually monarch of Rome.

§ **209.** This was C. Sempronius Gracchus, younger brother of Tiberius, already conspicuous as one of the Commissioners under Tiberius' law. *C. Gracchus.* Nine years younger than his brother, and like him full of designs for reforming the state, Gaius had no need to hunt for popularity. He had served in Spain under Scipio in 133 B.C., and as quaestor in Sardinia in 126 B.C. On his return from that province without authorization (124 B.C.), he was impeached by the senate for complicity in the revolt at Fregellae, but acquitted. All men knew that he had come back to resume his brother's work, and he was elected tribune for 123 B.C.

The constitution of Rome had proved itself incapable of preventing the abuses which follow from the quarrel of the few rich with the many poor. Once a republic of equal citizens, Rome had become now an oligarchy of the most exclusive kind. Gaius set himself to accomplish two objects: to overthrow the oligarchy, and to *His aims.* better the lot of the poorer citizens. His brother had aimed at the latter only, but Gaius was a political as well as a social reformer.

§ **210.** Ten years after his brother's first tribunate he

brought forward a series of measures calculated to win the support against the senate of the various classes who had grievances demanding redress. The order in which his proposal was introduced is not known, nor again can we be sure of the year, for Gaius was elected to a second tribunate in 122 B.C., and no doubt continued to press forward and develop his schemes.

Legislation of C. Gracchus, 123, 122 B.C.

(i) A *lex frumentaria* decreed that the state should provide corn once a month to all citizens at a price less than half its market value.

(ii) The *lex agraria* of Tiberius Gracchus was renewed but not re-enforced.

(iii) Colonies were to be established at Tarentum and elsewhere in Italy, besides one at Carthage (*Iunonia*), which was to include poor Italians.

(iv) A series of army-reforms was introduced: all citizens on service were to have the right of appeal from an officer's capital sentence; the soldier's clothing was henceforth to be found in addition to his pay; no one was to be called for military service except between the ages of seventeen and forty-five; a foot-soldier after serving sixteen campaigns, a horse-soldier after ten, was to be free from liability to further service.

(v) In addition to the existing permanent Commission for Extortion (*de repetundis*), others were to be established for the trial of cases of poisoning and murder, and the jurymen in all these courts were to be chosen from the equestrian order.

(vi) The taxes of Asia were to be put up for auction at Rome instead of being collected by the provincials themselves.

(vii) Before the election of consuls for any year, the senate was to decide what provinces should be assigned to them.

Tendency of these Laws.

The first of these laws secured the support of the proletariate, but it was fraught with the most pernicious consequences, for it increased the depopulation of the country districts by teaching the dregs of the country folk to flock to Rome, where bread was to be had for the asking. The second law Gaius appears to have proposed rather as a tribute to his brother's memory than because he desired to re-open the question of allotments. The third is remarkable as being the forerunner of that colonization beyond the sea which afterwards became a recognized feature of the democratic programme. By far the most important is the fifth. Gaius saw that he needed firmer support than the proletariate could afford him: accordingly he destroyed the union which had previously existed between the senate and the Equites, by raising the latter to a position of **rivalry** in the state. The control which the senate had hitherto possessed over the law-courts was taken from them and handed over to the merchants and money-lenders of the **equestrian order.** In other words, the Equites were bribed to take Gaius' side by the prospect of plundering the provinces; for if any senatorial governor endeavoured to prevent their **extortion** he did so at the peril of having a charge **trumped up** against him by the Equites, and being condemned by them in the court where they acted as jurors. The sixth law was also intended to gratify the Equites, for **Asia was the** richest of the provinces, and presented an almost unlimited field for their malpractices.

§ **211.** Thus Gaius had not fallen into the error, which his brother had committed, of relying upon **one** section of the community only. He had the *Proposal of Gracchus about the Franchise.* starving proletariate to back him up indeed, but he had also the great financial magnates of the state. Unfortunately a further law which **he proposed** in order to win over the Latins and Italians, viz.:—

(viii) That the full franchise should be granted to the Latins, and Latin rights to the allies;

broke up the coalition. His motive no doubt was to soothe the Italians for any loss that might befall them through the establishment of the colonies at Tarentum and elsewhere; but as in the time of Flaccus, the populace objected to sharing their comitial privileges with any new-comers, and they began to fall away from their leader.

The senate saw its opportunity: it would widen the coldness into a quarrel by pretending to become the patron of the poor. A tribune, M. Livius Drusus, was prompted to propose laws—

Counter-proposals of M. Livius Drusus, 122 B.C.

(*a*) That the small rent-charge for land allotted by the law of the elder Gracchus should be remitted, and that the allotments should be henceforth free and transferable.

(*b*) That twelve colonies of 3000 citizens each should be established for the benefit of the poor, not beyond the seas but in Italy.

Gaius was at the time absent, superintending his new colony at Junonia; when he returned it was too late. He was not elected to the tribunate of 121 B.C., and L. Opimius, his most active foe, was chosen consul.

§ 212. Immediately upon the commencement of the consular year, Opimius proposed the abolition of Junonia, having previously worked upon the scruples of the people by aid of the priests, and by the report of awful portents and ill omens connected with the accursed spot. Gaius appeared in the Forum, and one of his supporters struck down Antullius, a sacrificial servant, for some insulting language. A riot ensued, and the senate at once ordered Opimius to assume the powers of a dictator—*videret ne quid detrimenti respublica caperet*, "let him see that the state received no harm." He armed senators and slaves and the few Equites who held by the senate, occupied the Capitol, and on the following morning advanced to the Aventine, where Gaius' supporters were collected. Gaius himself endeavoured to obviate a collision, and M. Fulvius Flaccus, now as ever faithful to the popular cause, sent his son to treat with the senate. The latter arrested young Flaccus, and offered its weight in gold for the head of either Gaius or Flaccus the elder. In the attack on the Aventine the mob was speedily dispersed. Gaius would

Fall of C. Gracchus, 121 B.C.

have stood his ground but was persuaded **to fly**. His body was found in the grove of **Furinna with that of one slave**, who had slain his master by command and then himself.

§ **213**. When Gaius fell the popular party was left without a head. **His** adherents to the number of three thousand were mercilessly tracked out by a special commission under L. Opimius, and **the** populace made **no** resistance. Too debased to be loyal, they only cared **to** get as much as **they** could, and **they** now looked to the tribune Drusus to fulfil his promises. But he had only acted as the instrument of the senate, and **the** senate had no mind to fulfil promises of which the purpose was already served. On **the contrary** it attacked **in detail** every act of Gaius' tribunate and gradually **recovered most of** its power. The question of the *iudicia* alone gave it serious trouble. Yet the memory of the revolution did not die. The mob had learnt its powers: **it** was sovereign, and could, at will, interfere with every department of government; all that the senate could do was to cajole it and see that none stepped forward to lead it.

<small>The Oligarchic Reaction.</small>

§ **214**. The land laws were first **attacked**. The decree prohibiting any further attempt **to** refound Carthage (*Junonia*) was carried, and shortly after were cancelled all other transmarine colonies. One only **held** its ground, and struggled on until it became a great city, Narbo (*Narbonne*) in Gaul; but, as will be seen, this was because of its utility from a military point of view. Gaius' Italian colonies fared no better; while the twelve promised by Drusus were allowed to be forgotten. The commission for distributing lands, restored by Gaius, existed nominally until 119 B.C., when Spurius Thorius, prompted **by** the senate, passed **a law that** all remaining public land should be left to its present occupiers **for a**

<small>Fate of the Land Laws.</small>

small rental, which was to go towards the fund for the provision of corn. Finally in 111 B.C. a new law decreed that this small tax should be abolished and that all holdings should be alienable. Thus the smaller and poorer tenants were soon bought out or evicted by less honourable means: the entire domain land passed again into the hands of the wealthy, who were exempted from any payment for their possessions. All the labours of the Gracchi were lost. Grass-farming and slave-labour grew up anew, and the depopulation of Italy became every year more marked.

The corn-laws the senate dared not touch, yet even in the popular party the wiser men saw that such laws were radically evil. Their sole tendency was to encourage pauperism and discourage labour, to fill Rome with beggars who would sell their support for a fresh largess. The famous Gaius Marius endeavoured in his tribunate (119 B.C.) to curtail these distributions, but without success.

The Corn-Laws.

The Equites were long left unmolested in their new powers. With regard to the jury-courts, the senatorial party came to a tacit understanding with the Equites, that the latter should be allowed to plunder the provinces at will, and should in turn suffer the senatorial governors to share what remained. The provinces had reason to regret the transfer of the *iudicia* to the new class. Before this they had had but their governors to fear: now they had governors and Equites as well.

The iudicia.

In fine, the one feature of the Gracchan reform which might have produced good results—the design of providing lands by allotment and colonization, and so re-peopling Italy—was abolished; and every feature that was faulty and dangerous, the corn-doles and the abuse of justice, was fostered by the restored nobles. There set in "an age of political mediocrities," for it was the policy of the aristocrats to distribute office and power amongst the younger members of their own ranks, and not to encourage the rise of men of mark such as had been Scipio and Paulus. Hence came disaster and disgrace on all hands abroad, corruption and intrigue at home. The next great names in Roman history are those of men who attained power by aid of the populace.

§ 215. The conquest of Liguria and the other tribes beyond the Padus (*Po*) was completed in 143 B.C., when Appius Claudius reduced the Salassi and took from them the gold-washings of Victumulae. Between Spain and Italy, however, there was no means of communication except by sea, for in Gaul only Massilia was in alliance with Rome. It was manifestly to be desired that the provinces in Spain should be connected more closely with Italy. Accordingly, when in 125 B.C. the senate were anxious to be rid of M. Fulvius Flaccus, the partisan of the Gracchi, they sent him into Gaul to secure a footing for the Romans in that quarter.

Wars in Gallia Transalpina.

The country between the Rhone and the Alps as far as the Isara (*Isère*) was occupied by the Salluvii and Vocontii, tribes of mixed Ligurian and Celtic descent; while beyond these lay the more important Gallic tribes of the Allobroges and the Aedui. The whole region east of the Rhone was fertile and its inhabitants were but weak. Beyond the Rhone the power of Gaul lay with the Arverni in Auvergne, and so formidable were they that the Aedui (about *Autun*) and the Suessiones (near *Soissons*) in the north were their only rivals. Flaccus campaigned successfully (125, 124 B.C.) against the Salluvii and Vocontii; his successor C. Sextius Calvinus defeated the Allobroges who came to the assistance of the Salluvii (123, 122 B.C.); and Cn. Domitius Ahenobarbus, following up these successes, forced the Allobroges in their turn to summon the Arverni to their aid. The Arvernian king Betuitus brought up 180,000 men to help the Gauls, and the senate despatched the consul Q. Fabius Maximus, 121 B.C., to support Ahenobarbus. In a great battle at the junction of the Rhone and the Isère in that year, the Arverni were utterly routed with, it is said, the loss of 150,000 men, mostly drowned in their flight across the Rhone. The Allobroges submitted at once. Soon afterwards Ahenobarbus captured Betuitus by treachery, and in the battle of Vindalium near Avennio (*Avignon*) reduced the Arverni to peace (121 B.C.). The country from the Lake of Geneva to the Pyrenees was constituted a province, called Gallia Narbonensis from its chief town of Narbo, where three years later (118 B.C.) was established a colony. Communication with Spain was thus secured. Narbo (*Narbonne*) was colonized partly as a concession to the populace, as some fulfilment of the promises of Livius Drusus, partly as a garrison town for the new province, partly in the interests of the Equites as a commercial rival to Massilia. The town of Aquae Sextiae (*Aix*) sprung up where C. Sextius had fixed his head-quarters.

The Province of Gallia Narbonensis.

§ **216.** When Massinissa of Numidia died, 149 B.C., his kingdom was divided between his three sons; Micipsa was the acknowledged king, but Gulussa, who sent troops to act at the siege of Carthage, was commander-in-chief, and Mastanabal was entrusted with the control of justice. Both the younger brothers died before 118 B.C., and Micipsa, whose death occurred in that year, left his kingdom to be divided between

Jugurthine War, 111 B.C.—105 B.C.

his own sons Adherbal and Hiempsal, and his nephew Jugurtha, son of Mastanabal. Jugurtha had led a contingent of Numidians to the aid of Scipio in the Numantine war, and besides distinguishing himself by his courage, had intrigued so successfully with many of the leading Romans that he could count upon their support in the future. Now left co-heir with Micipsa's sons, he refused to be satisfied with his share of the kingdom, assassinated Hiempsal (117 B.C.), and forced Adherbal to fly to Rome. The senate divided Numidia between Adherbal and Jugurtha, and a commission under L. Opimius, which was sent to carry out the arrangement, gave the capital, Cirta (*Constantine*), to Adherbal, while the western and more productive region fell to Jugurtha. Five years passed, during which Jugurtha, confident of the connivance of the Romans, continued to harass his adopted brother. Eventually he shut him up in the almost impregnable city of Cirta, 112 B.C., and declined to pay any attention to an embassy of young nobles which was despatched by the senate to interfere. A third commission under M. Aemilius Scaurus, the leader of the aristocracy, was no more successful, and while the senate still hesitated Cirta fell. The inhabitants, many of them Roman and Italian traders, were put to death, and Adherbal was killed by torture (112 B.C.). Whereupon Jugurtha sent envoys to explain his action and to purchase the acquiescence of the senate.

<small>Fall of Cirta, 112 B.C.</small>

He was now in possession of the entire kingdom of his grandfather Massinissa, a kingdom stretching from the borders of Egypt on the east to those of Mauretania, the kingdom of Bocchus, on the west, excepting only the Roman province about the site of Carthage. He had a full treasury, an inexhaustible supply of men, and his

Numidians were the finest light cavalry in the world. He had married the daughter of Bocchus, whom he might therefore consider his ally.

§ **217.** The senate, after vain endeavours to ignore Adherbal's fate, was compelled by the popular indignation and the harangues of C. Memmius, tribune designate, to declare war. The consul L. Calpurnius Bestia, and his legate Scaurus, entered Africa, and when Bocchus appeared likely to support them, Jugurtha offered terms. He purchased a peace which left him in possession of his kingdom at the price of a petty fine and the surrender of his elephants (111 B.C.).

<small>Campaign of L. Calpurnius Bestia, 111 B.C.</small>

In Rome there was deep anger at the treaty. The senators were again threatened with impeachment by the tribune C. Memmius, and were constrained to summon Jugurtha to defend himself in person, granting him safe-conduct. The king came, bought over one of the tribunes whose veto defeated the purpose of Memmius, and finding that his kinsman Massiva, a son of Gulussa, was suing for restoration, had him assassinated at Rome by an agent named Bomilcar. Whereupon the people forced the senate to cancel the peace and dismiss the king; Sp. Postumius Albinus was entrusted with the command against him.

Sp. Albinus did nothing, for his army was too much demoralized to be serviceable. He left Africa at the close of 110 B.C., passing on the command to his brother Aulus. This general coveted the wealth of Jugurtha, and marched upon his treasure city of Suthul (*Guelma*). The attack failed; the legions, induced by a simulated retreat to follow the king into the desert, were suddenly beset by the entire Numidian army, and lost their camp. The Romans were forced to purchase their lives by passing under the yoke, and by agreeing

<small>Defeat of Aulus Albinus, 109 B.C.</small>

to evacuate Numidia forthwith and renew the peace of Scaurus (109 B.C.).

§ **218**. Thereupon C. Mamilius Limetanus, tribune, secured the appointment of a special commission (*quaestio Limetana*) to try the senatorial leaders on charges of high treason and corruption. A number were exiled, amongst them Sp. Albinus and L. Opimius, the adversary of C. Gracchus. Scaurus contrived to get himself made president of the commission, and thus saved himself at the expense of fellow criminals not more guilty. The second treaty was cancelled; Q. Caecilius Metellus (the nephew of that Metellus who crushed the pretender Andriscus in Macedonia) was put in command, and amongst his lieutenants was C. Marius, who as tribune in 119 B.C., had made an attack upon the corn-doles. Metellus was a good general, and if he had little scruple on other points, he was at least proof against bribery. Energetic measures reorganized the army, and a great battle on the river Muthul, in which the safety of the Romans was due in large part to the valour of Marius, gave to the invaders possession of the greater part of Numidia. Most of the towns surrendered, but Jugurtha shut himself up in Cirta, and Zama successfully withstood a short siege, during which Metellus' camp was taken (end of 109 B.C.).

The Quaestio Limetana.

First campaign of Metellus, 109 B.C.

Jugurtha felt the danger of his position: he again attempted to negotiate terms, and surrendered much treasure and stores, and probably his capital Cirta; but when asked to surrender himself he refused, and broke off the negotiations. Metellus was sufficiently dishonourable to retain everything that had been given up, though Jugurtha had gained nothing in return. The Numidians, however, were still anxious to continue the struggle. The town of Vaga (*Beja*), which had opened its gates to the Romans, revolted anew and massacred the entire Roman garrison. Two days later it was recovered and paid the usual penalty, but the Numidian tribes still flocked to Jugurtha. The whole campaign of 108 B.C. was wasted in the idle effort to capture the king amidst his deserts. Moreover Bocchus the Mauretanian seemed not unlikely to aid him. He was afraid of Jugurtha's power, but still more afraid of the prospect of having the Romans as his neighbours.

<small>Second campaign, 108 B.C.</small>

§ **219.** At the close of the campaign of 108 B.C. Marius returned to Rome as a candidate for the consulship. He was only the son of a Sabine farmer of Arpinum; yet he found supporters enough, for he was a good soldier, and though no orator, was on good terms with the people. He was elected easily, and was appointed to the command in Africa for the campaign of 107 B.C.

<small>Election of Marius to the consulship for 107 B.C.</small>

The election of Marius was a serious blow to the aristocrats, for it marked the passing away from them of the monopoly of the higher magistracies. Without birth, money, or patronage, Marius attained by popular will the highest office in the state, and the precedent was not forgotten. A change introduced by Marius was no less momentous: heretofore service in the legions had depended, as had been the case ever since the Servian Reform, upon the possession of a certain amount of property, originally 11,000 *asses*, but subsequently lowered to 4000; Marius did away with this restriction, and threw open the ranks to the *capite censi*, that is, to those citizens on the tribal lists who had not even the lower of these two qualifications. The effect was disastrous in many ways: it opened the way to the formation of armies devoted to the interest of indulgent leaders, and so heralded the civil wars. But it was necessary in so far as there were scarce any left in Rome who possessed the amount of property requisite under the old system, and were at the same time desirous of military service.

During the year 107 B.C. Metellus still retained the command as proconsul while Marius was levying troops in Italy. It was not until late in the year that Marius appeared and took over the legions. When the new troops, who had as yet seen nothing of war, had been drilled sufficiently, Marius commenced operations by the surprise of Capsa (*Kafsa*), a very strong fortress, with whose fall the whole of eastern Numidia came into the hands of the Romans.

First campaign of Marius, 107 B.C.

§ 220. Next year, 106 B.C., Marius after a march of many hundred miles, reached the Muluchath (*Mejerdeh*), the border river between Numidia and Mauretania. Bocchus was alarmed by the progress of the Romans, and supported Jugurtha in the attempt to cut off their retreat. Marius was placed in great peril on at least three occasions during the backward march, and his escape he owed mainly to the courage and dash of L. Cornelius Sulla, his quaestor, who commanded the cavalry. At last he reached his headquarters at Cirta in safety and passed the winter there.

Second campaign of Marius, 106 B.C.

To conquer the Numidians in open war seemed a hopeless task and Marius had recourse to intrigue. Sulla served him well in the matter, and Bocchus was induced to betray Jugurtha, albeit his own son-in-law, as the price of the friendship of Rome. Jugurtha was invited to a conference, where he was surprised and surrendered in chains to Sulla (105 B.C.). Marius triumphed in the following year, though the

Capture of Jugurtha, 105 B.C.

T. R.   X

real work of the war had been done by Metellus and Sulla.¹ Although Numidia was thus at the mercy of the Romans it was not converted into a province. The western half was added to the kingdom of Bocchus, while the eastern was made over to Gauda, the half-witted brother of Jugurtha. Jugurtha perished by violence or starvation in the Tullianum at Rome, and while he lay dying the people summoned the conqueror to lead their legions against a far more formidable enemy, the Gauls and Germans of the North.

§ **221.** The Ligurian war, and the campaigns of Flaccus and his successors in Narbonese Gaul, had for their object the consolidation of the frontier on the north-west. A similar task kept various commanders occupied on the north-eastern frontier, about the head of the Adriatic and Illyricum. After the war with Teuta little or nothing was done in this direction until 184 B.C., when, on the rumour that Philip of Macedon meditated an invasion of Italy by land with the aid of the Thracian peoples, a colony was settled at Aquileia. Subsequently, when Macedonia became a province, it was found that this acquisition of territory brought the Romans into conflict with the more or less savage tribes who lived to the south of the Danube. Frontier wars of little importance were conducted almost without intermission from 150 B.C. onwards. In 114 B.C. a consul, C. Porcius Cato, and his army marched out of Macedonia and were cut to pieces by the Scordisci, a people dwelling in what is now called Servia. A war thus commenced which lasted until

Conflicts with the Northern Tribes.

---

¹ The chronology of the war from 109 B.C. to 106 B.C. is doubtful. The dates given here are from Ihne.

110 B.C., when M. Minucius penetrated to the Danube and finally crushed the Scordisci. Unfortunately by breaking the strength of this Danubian people, the Romans had destroyed the bulwark which had thus far protected them from a far more terrible foe. The Cimbri, or "the Champions," a people of Germanic origin, had long been hovering about the northern bank of the Danube, unable to force a southward passage in face of the brave Celtic tribes like the Scordisci by which the river was covered. Now the Cimbrian and Roman came face to face.

§ **222.** The Cimbri had much in common with the Gauls; they lived only for battle and deeds of valour, owned as king the bravest of their number, sacrificed to their gods their prisoners of war, and had little civilization. They moved along with no fixed homes, living in the wagons which accompanied them. In 113 B.C. they presented themselves at the passes of the Carnic Alps, close to the colony of Aquileia. They were met by Cn. Papirius Carbo, and ordered to quit the lands of the Taurisci, who were friends, that is dependents, of Rome. They obeyed, and Carbo treacherously drew them into an ambuscade. They revenged themselves by inflicting a terrible defeat on the faithless Roman, but instead of at once entering Italy, they passed westward over the Jura, and there lived quietly.

The Cimbri.

Defeat of Cn. Papirius Carbo, 113 B.C.

In this position, however, they appeared to threaten the newly-acquired province of Narbonese Gaul, and to protect this M. Junius Silanus brought up an army in 109 B.C. The Cimbri asked for lands in which to settle: Silanus retorted by attacking them, and lost both army and camp. It was most difficult to raise new troops to face these flaxen-haired giants, and the senate was relieved to find that the Cimbri contented

And of M. Junius Silanus, 109 B.C.

themselves with repeating their demand for lands, and refrained from any advance upon the Roman frontier.

§ **223.** But now a new foe appeared. The Helvetii, a Celtic tribe settled in Switzerland, grew restless, and advanced to seek less barren lands to the west of their Alpine homes. The consul L. Cassius Longinus encountered them near Agen on the Garonne, and fell with most of his troops (107 B.C.). The remainder of the army bought its safety by passing under the yoke, surrendering its baggage and hostages, and at once withdrawing. For this **treaty the** interim commander C. Popilius **was impeached on a charge of treason** and condemned to exile. Tolosa (*Toulouse*) now **revolted,** but was recovered by Q. Servilius **Caepio in** the following year, for neither Cimbri nor Helvetii showed any desire to molest those who did not provoke them. At Tolosa Caepio improved his opportunity by plundering the great temple of the Celtic Apollo, 106 B.C.

The Helvetii.

In 105 B.C. there were three armies in Gaul to meet the Cimbri, who, under their king Boiorix, now made a definite advance upon Italy. M. Aurelius Scaurus, an ex-consul, was the first victim : **completely routed on** the eastern bank of the Rhone, he was captured and put to death for the haughty spirit with **which he** answered his captors. The consul Cn. Mallius Maximus now summoned Caepio, the proconsul, from the western bank, and the combined armies **lay side** by side at **Arausio (***Orange***),** to the number of more than 80,000 Romans, exclusive of auxiliaries and other troops. The two commanders quarrelled, and despite the entreaties of the senate persisted in their antagonism. The chief command **of course belonged to** the consul Maximus, and this galled the pride of Caepio, who ventured to attack the Cimbri single-handed so as to forestall his colleague in the expected victory. His army perished almost to a man, his camp was taken, and the victorious Cimbri followed up one triumph by another scarcely less complete over Maximus (Oct. 6, 105 B.C.). The dead numbered 120,000, of whom two-thirds were Romans. No such defeat had been experienced since the fatal day of Cannae; but, though the road to Italy was open, the Cimbri passed on towards Spain.

Battle of Arausio, 105 B.C.

The people promptly showed its indignation against Caepio: he was at once deprived of his imperium, his property was confiscated, and his seat in the senate taken from him. There were other symptoms of the popular restlessness. By the *Lex Domitia* of 104 B.C., vacancies in the priestly colleges were no longer filled by co-optation but by the vote of seventeen of the tribes chosen by lot. C. Marius was returned a second time as consul for 104 B.C.

§ **224.** His triumph over, **Marius left** Rome forthwith, and took up the command of what troops were left in the Narbonese, 104 B.C. He carried with him a number of new levies raised in Italy by the extraordinary measures of the consul P. Rutilius Rufus in 105 B.C., when so great was the panic, that it had been necessary to forbid any man capable of military service to leave the country. With these, assisted by contingents from Massilia, the Allobroges, and other peoples of the Transalpine districts who dreaded the Cimbri no less than did the Romans, Marius was able to put the Narbonese in a good state of defence. The Cimbri meantime had entered Spain and had been driven out by the stubborn valour of the Celtiberi. In 103 B.C. they passed northward along the western shore of Gaul up to

Second consulship of Marius, 104 B.C.

the Seine, and were there joined by other German hordes, notably the Teutones. Failing to oust the Belgae of northern Gaul, they once more wheeled about and advanced upon Italy by two routes. The Cimbri made for the passes of the Carnic Alps; the Teutones and Ambrones were to enter Italy by the western roads.

§ 225. Marius had returned for a space to Rome towards the end of 104 B.C. to hold the consular comitia, and had been a third time returned as consul. He employed the year (103 B.C.) as before in preparing the province and his army for the impending struggle. When at last it came (102 B.C.) he was consul for the fourth time, with Q. Lutatius Catulus, an aristocrat, as his colleague. He entrenched himself at the juncture of the Rhone and Isara (*Isère*), and suffered the Teutones and Ambrones to cross the stream and attack his camp without assuming the offensive. The Germans knew nothing of sieges, and soon gave up the task of storming the Roman position. As they passed on towards the Alps, Marius followed cautiously. He overtook them near Aquae Sextiae (*Aix*), where he again entrenched himself upon a hill after a successful skirmish with the Ambrones. Two days later the barbarians attempted to storm his position, and for half the day the fight was obstinate. Then the Germans broke and fled to their baggage-waggons whither the legions followed them. The entire host was annihilated, men, women, and children alike. The victory of Marius was complete, and when he returned to Rome he was chosen consul for the fifth time.

Battle of Aquae Sextiae, 102 B.C.

Meanwhile the second horde, the Cimbri, guided and swelled by the Helvetii, had traversed the Brenner Pass and descended the eastern bank of the Athesis (*Adige*) towards the Po. They were encountered by Catulus, the second consul, with a full army; but so great was the terror of their name that at first sight of the enemy the legions broke and fled. With difficulty Catulus retreated to the southern bank of the **Po, thus** leaving all Transpadane Gaul at the mercy of the invaders.

In the spring of 101 B.C. he was joined by Marius, now a fifth time consul, and the two commanders crossed the Po and marched eastwards towards Vercellae (*Vercelli*). At a spot called Campi Raudii they fell unexpectedly upon the Germans. The Cimbri were annihilated as completely as the Teutones had **been.** Few survived to be the slaves of their conquerors. **Henceforth Rome** had no German invaders to fear until the days when Alaric led **his Goths into** Italy.

_{Battle of Vercellae, 101 B.C.}

§ **226.** While the deadly contest **with the northern tribes** was in progress, Rome **was harassed by** a servile war. The scene **of** the uprising was Sicily, where gangs of slaves, starved, overworked and tortured, toiled on the land chained **neck to neck.** They had broken out into revolt once **before in 135 B.C.,** under the leadership of Eunus, a Syrian juggler **who gave himself** the title of King Antiochus, and of his lieutenants Cleon and Achaeus. At one time they were in possession **of the** important towns of Messana and Agrigentum, and were not crushed until P. Rupilius, the consul of 132 B.C., took their strongholds, Enna and Tauromenium (*Taormina*), and crucified 20,000 of his prisoners.

_{First Sicilian Slave War.}

In 104 B.C. P. Licinius Nerva, the praetor of Sicily, held a court in Syracuse to inquire into the condition of persons who, though belonging to nations **in alliance** with Rome, had been captured by the slave-merchants and **sold** into captivity. Nerva ordered the release of no fewer than 800, but when the numbers of those demanding

_{Second Sicilian Slave War.}

redress continually increased, he grew alarmed at the prevalent excitement and refused to hear any further cases. This was the signal for insurrection: in the east of the island a Syrian magician, Salvius, who assumed the title of King Tryphon, defeated Nerva near Morgantia; while in the west a Cilician, **Athenio**, a man of considerable ability, gathered a force and placed it under the command of King Tryphon. The slaves held their ground for the next two years, despite the fact that they had to contend against considerable bodies of troops, and it was not until 101 B.C., when the consul M'. Aquillius took the command, that Athenio, now general through the death of Tryphon, was defeated in a great battle and the revolt so came to an end.

§ **227.** Since the fall of C. Gracchus the popular party had been without a great leader. Nevertheless it was not crushed. The disasters, corruption, and general misgovernment of the restored senate had only aroused the democrats to renewed efforts, and they had shown their indignation by the prosecution of the incapable generals who had commanded against Jugurtha and the Sicilian slaves. What they needed was a leader with force to back his efforts. As they thought, they had found the necessary man in Marius, who owed his five consulships to them, and who came back from the field of Vercellae in 101 B.C. at the head of a victorious army absolutely devoted to his interests. Accordingly, Saturninus and Glaucia, the heads of the popular party, entered into an alliance with the great general, and in return for his support secured for him a sixth consulship.

The Coalition of Marius, Saturninus, and Glaucia.

L. Appuleius Saturninus had already held office: in 104 B.C. he had been quaestor, but his management of the corn-supplies was distasteful to the senate and he was superseded, an insult which caused him to join the popular party. When tribune in 103 B.C., he passed or proposed several laws in the interests of the democracy, notably one that sanctioned the distribution of land in Africa among the veterans of Marius, and another relating to high treason (*maiestas*), which was brought in to ensure the inviolability of the tribunes. He found a strenuous and able ally in C. Servilius Glaucia, who seems by no means entirely to deserve the charge of low cunning and low wit which writers of contrary views brought against him. He had won prominence by supporting the claims of the Equites to the jury-courts, of which it seems they were for a time deprived by a law of Q. Servilius Caepio, the defeated general of Arausio. Metellus, the conqueror of Jugurtha, endeavoured during his censorship (102 B.C.) to eject both Saturninus and Glaucia from the senate, but his colleague disapproved of so violent a proceeding. In the elections for 100 B.C. Marius, Saturninus, and Glaucia were candidates for the consulship, tribunate, and praetorship respectively. The soldiery of Marius were present in ample numbers, and Marius and Glaucia obtained the offices they desired. Saturninus however would have failed had not his partisans openly murdered Nonius, who was on the point of being returned for the tenth and last vacancy in the tribunician college.

§ **228.** Saturninus proposed—

(i) That the Gallic lands recently occupied by the Cimbri, which by the law of war were now at the disposal of the state, should be distributed among new Roman colonies, and that any senator who refused to swear obedience to the law within five days should be expelled from the senate.

The Leges Appuleiae, 100 B.C.

(ii) That colonies (probably open to Italians) should be established in Transalpine Gaul, Sicily, Achaea, and Macedonia.

(iii) That corn should be sold by the state at a lower rate than even that fixed by C. Gracchus.

The first of these laws was proposed chiefly to gratify Marius, for the bulk of the new colonists would be his old soldiers, and he would himself receive extensive powers for settling the colonies. The corn law of course conciliated the proletariate. The senate offered what resistance it could, but the combination of army, Italians, and populace was too powerful: the tribunes who vetoed the laws were driven from the place of voting, and the proposals were carried by sheer force. When the senators were called upon to swear to obey the agrarian law, Marius at first declared that he would not take the oath, afterwards however he said that he would obey it so far as it was law—that is, in accordance with the constitution. Metellus Numidicus alone absolutely refused and went into banishment, to the great joy, as people said, of Marius, whose mortal foe he had been since the time when (108 B.C.) he had attempted to prevent the candidature of the latter for the consulship. Before the year was over the alliance between the three politicians was sorely shaken: the proletariate disliked the colonial law; the Equites, whose interests were solely on the side of law and order, were disgusted by the late scenes of violence; and finally Marius, altogether lost amid the storms of the Forum, fell more and more away from his friends.

§ **229.** Saturninus and Glaucia were too deeply involved to desist. They had no choice but to secure re-election or to submit to prosecution. Accordingly Saturninus offered himself for a third tribunate, Glaucia for the consulship, for which he was legally unqualified. On the day of the consular elections they saw that C. Memmius, once the agitator in the

Death of Saturninus and Glaucia.

Jugurthine war, but now the senatorial candidate, would be returned, and they had him murdered. But the senate was prepared: the nobles and their adherents armed for the struggle, and invested Marius sorely against his will with dictatorial powers. On the day following Saturninus gave regular battle in the Forum to the senatorial party. The latter easily prevailed. The democrats fled to the Capitol, and there capitulated when the water-supply was cut off. Marius confined their leaders in the senate-house, hoping that they would thus be safe; but before any decision could be arrived at with regard to their punishment, the young nobles pulled open the roof and stoned them to death. The senators followed up their victory by the recall of Metellus. Marius, who had ruined the popular party by his indecision, retired in disgust to Asia, awaiting a new opportunity for the display of his military genius.

§ 230. This decisive victory of the senate secured tranquillity for a period of ten years, broken only by two noteworthy incidents. In 95 B.C., by a *Lex Licinia-Mucia*, Latins and Italians resident in Rome were ordered to leave the capital. The law was enforced, but at the cost of civil war, for it was this enactment, as much as any other event, that drove the Italians into the struggle of a few years later. In 92 B.C. the Equestrian order showed once more that it was determined to use its control of the jury-courts for the oppression of the provincials. P. Rutilius Rufus, the legate of the noble Q. Mucius Scaevola in Asia, had repressed in his province with a stern hand the extortion of the *publicani* and their agents. In revenge, he was charged with extortion, and condemned by an unscrupulous Equestrian jury. The falsity of the accusation was sufficiently proved by the reception which the provincials gave Rufus when he went

The Exile of Rutilius Rufus, 92 B.C.

into exile in Asia. He was welcomed with every mark of affection by the very people he was declared to have plundered.

§ **231.** At length there appeared another reformer, this time from the ranks of the aristocracy. M.

Proposals of M. Livius Drusus, 91 B.C.

Livius Drusus, who was the son of the opponent of C. Gracchus, desired to do justice to the provincials and at the same time to strengthen the senate by depriving the Equites of their judicial powers; to win over the populace by corn and land laws; and to give the franchise to the Italians. He proposed—

(i) That the *iudicia* should be transferred to the senate, which was to be increased by 300 new members.
(ii) That cheap corn should be distributed.
(iii) That the remnant of the public land, notably that in Campania, should be allotted to new colonists.
(iv) [A proposal kept back for the present] That the full franchise should be extended to the Italians.

The Equites opposed him furiously, and while many of the better sort of senators gave him their support, there was a large party which preferred to share the plunder of the provinces with the Equites, and so was hostile. Chief among these latter was the Consul Philippus. It was clearly impossible to carry the laws separately, for the populace, though anxious for colonies, would not have supported the measure for depriving the Equites of their judicial powers; therefore Drusus, despite a law passed a few years before, put them to the vote in a body, and arrested the consul when he attempted to break off the polling. By this means all three laws were passed; but Philippus declared them illegally carried, and it seemed that he would unite with the Equites to use force. The timid senators gave way; the promise which Drusus had made to the Italians became known, and cries of traitor were raised. The reformer was left alone, or supported only by the Italians, and his laws were cancelled by the very senate for which he acted. A few days later he was assassinated. The Italians, once again disappointed, would wait no longer. Drusus' murder was the signal for the Social War.

§ 232. The victorious party declared that Drusus was in treasonable correspondence with the Italians, and by a *Lex Varia*, 91 B.C., a special commission was appointed to try the most prominent of his followers. Angered anew by this attack on their friends, the Italians broke out into revolt. The people of Asculum (*Ascoli*) in Picenum led the way by the massacre of a Roman praetor and his attendants. Marsi, Paeligni, Marrucini, Vestini and the tribes of Samnium joined in the insurrection until all central and southern Italy was in arms. Only in Etruria, Umbria and Campania, where the great landowners were strongest, did the Romans hold their own. Corfinium (*Pentima*), a Paelignian town, was selected as the capital of the new confederation. A senate of 500, two consuls, twelve praetors were chosen; a curia and forum were built, and a new coinage was issued. Of the rebel consuls, the Marsian Q. Pompaedius Silo held the north and centre of the peninsula; while the other, the Samnite C. Papius Mutilus, was commander-in-chief of Italy from Campania southwards. The Roman consuls opposed respectively to them were P. Rutilius Lupus and L. Julius Caesar.

[sidenote: The Social War, 90 B.C.—88 B.C.]

The first attack of the Romans was directed against the revolted town of Asculum. Cn. Pompeius Strabo was here in command against the insurgents, and after serious reverses was able to besiege the place in earnest.

[sidenote: First Campaign, 90 B.C.]

The consul Rutilius Lupus who took the chief command in the north, lost the bulk of his men in surprises and battles when assailing the Marsi, and was at last slain. His successor was as unfortunate, and it was only when Marius, hitherto serving in a subordinate capacity, took the command that the Romans made any headway.

In southern and central Italy, the Romans were even less successful. The colonies throughout the land were now as in the Hannibalic war faithful to their mother city; but Aesernia, Beneventum, and Venusia were at once beset by the confederates, and the two first soon fell. The consul Caesar was beaten in Samnium. His legate, Crassus, was shut up in the Lucanian Grumentum (*Saponara*) and there forced to surrender. Encouraged by these successes, Mutilus overran all Campania as far as Vesuvius.

§ **233**. Thus the results of the first campaign were altogether favourable to the insurgents. The Romans were not sure of any part of the country beyond Latium and northern Campania, for at the close of the year the Etruscan and Umbrian towns revolted and could only be coerced by armed force. For the moment fear did away with party feeling at Rome, and the first sign of this was a motion carried by the tribune, M. Plautius Silvanus, which transferred the Commission on High Treason from the Equites to a jury elected by the tribes, and so ended the spiteful prosecutions in which the moneyed men had thus far indulged. The first victim of the new arrangement was the author of the Commission, Q. Varius. Then the burgesses began to think of compromise with the insurgents. At the close of 90 B.C. the consul L. Caesar carried a *Lex Iulia* to confer the franchise upon every Italian community which had not yet joined the secessionists, and the tribunes, the

The Lex Julia and Lex Plautia-Papiria.

above-mentioned Plautius and C. Papirius Carbo, passed another bill (the *Lex Plautia-Papiria*) that any resident of an Italian township who presented himself before a Roman magistrate within two months' date might so acquire the franchise. There was however one important qualification: the new voters were to be registered in eight tribes only. It was a bitter recantation for the selfish citizens, but it was one that was necessary in order to check the spread of revolt. It was politic too, for it offered rewards to all those Italians who deserted the national cause: it spread distrust amongst their ranks and so broke a power never too strongly concentrated.

§ 234. The new year (89 B.C.) opened with a general attack by the Romans. The consuls Cn. Pompeius Strabo and L. Porcius Cato both took command in the northern district, the former, as previously, in Picenum, the latter against the Marsi. L. Caesar, as proconsul, acted in the south, supported by Sulla and Cosconius. After a brave resistance Asculum was stormed by Pompeius, and with the fall of this important place came the submission of the surrounding peoples, the Vestini, Marrucini, and Paeligni. Progress was still more rapid in the south, where Cosconius quickly recovered all Apulia. Sulla, now commander of Caesar's army—for the pro-consul died early in the year—overran Campania, defeated and slew L. Cluentius before Nola and advanced into Samnium. He captured and sacked Aeclanum (*Mirabella*), defeated Mutilus and shut him up in Aesernia (*Isernia*), and took Bovianum (*Boiano*). The Hirpini now made peace: all Campania, except Nola and a few other isolated positions, had already been recovered, while the stronghold of the revolt, Samnium, maintained but the one fortress of Aesernia where the Italian senate was collected.

The Second Campaign, 89 B.C.

§ **235**. In 88 B.C. Pompaedius took over the supreme command of the remnant of the insurgents, but his forces **were reduced to 30,000** men, and even the arming of all the slaves who joined him only added 20,000 to this number. In spite of this, he contrived to recover Bovianum (*Boiano*), but fell soon afterwards in a skirmish. The war dragged on for a few months longer, but it had lost all serious proportions: Nola indeed withstood the assaults of three Roman armies, and **the Samnites**, who were still holding out amongst their own hills, **were not conquered** until seven years later, 82 B.C. But the *Lex Iulia* and the *Lex Plautia-Papiria* had done their work; and a *Lex Pompeia* of 89 B.C., which conferred upon the inhabitants of Gallia north of the Po the privileges before belonging to the Latins, the *Ius Latii*, completed the disarming of the country.

The Third Campaign, 88 B.C.

The result of the war was that the Latins and the bulk of the Italians received the full franchise, but the requisite journey to Rome to take part in the elections could be made **only by** the richer of them, and by the rabble who had no ties to keep them in their native towns, and who hoped at Rome to **earn a living by** the help of the corn-doles and by the sale of the votes with which they were now presented. The numerous middle class could not neglect their home duties for the journey, and as mentioned above, the Italians were only registered in eight of the thirty-five tribes, so that their political influence was not great. But **a great step had** been gained: the war cost 300,000 lives; but it added 80,000 new citizens to the census-roll, and it prepared **the way** for the enfranchisement of the provincials, which was soon to commence.

Result of the War.

§ **236**. The close of the social war inaugurated fresh

§ 236.] P. SULPICIUS RUFUS. 321

party conflicts in Rome. Finance was in disorder; the Italians resented their restriction to eight only of the tribes; Marius was angry because his rival Sulla had received the conduct of the war now afoot with Mithradates. Taking advantage of these elements of discontent, the tribune P. Sulpicius Rufus, a distinguished orator and soldier of the aristocratic party, proposed—

The Laws of P. Sulpicius Rufus, 88 B.C.

(i) That the Italians should be enrolled in all the thirty-five tribes.
(ii) That the sympathizers with the Italian cause who had been exiled by the Varian Commission should be recalled.
(iii) That the command in the East should be given to Marius.

The two consuls L. Cornelius Sulla and Q. Pompeius Rufus joined the senate in opposing these changes; but the Italians thronged the streets of Rome when the voting came on, and the Sulpician laws were carried amid violent riots in which Sulla all but lost his life. His army was encamped before Nola, and to it he at once hurried. He told his 35,000 men of the proceedings of Sulpicius, and inquired what was their will. They replied by tearing in pieces the tribunes who were sent to take the command from their general, and by marching upon the capital. Marius could levy no adequate force to resist, and when Sulla made his way into Rome almost without opposition, he fled with his chief partisans. Himself, Sulpicius, and ten others of their party were proscribed, and rewards were offered for their heads. Sulpicius was taken at Laurentum and his head was nailed to the Rostra. Marius was arrested as he lay hid in the marshes of Minturnae, but the German slave who was commissioned to execute him, had not the courage to slay the conqueror of the Cimbri. So he was suffered to escape, and fled to the island of Cercina (*Kerkenah*) in the bay of Tunis.

§ **237**. Sulla, instead of making himself monarch of

Rome, preferred to rehabilitate the senate, and to leave it to maintain peace and order while he himself restored Roman supremacy in the East. He at once annulled the Sulpician laws, and passed the following series of measures in the senatorial interest—

Measures of Sulla, 88 B.C.

(i) The senate was increased by 300 members of the Optimate party.
(ii) No magistrate should propose a bill to the people without first obtaining the assent (*auctoritas*) of the senate.
(iii) Votes on laws should be taken in the Comitia Centuriata (perhaps re-arranged on the Servian basis) instead of in the Comitia Tributa.

Of these measures, the second completely broke the power of the tribunes to introduce revolutionary and democratic bills, while the third transferred all ascendancy in the assembly to the rich. Events however prevented either from being carried out. Sulla, in spite of all his power, did not secure the election of his nominees to the consulship, for the choice of the people fell upon Cn. Octavius, an Optimate, and L. Cornelius Cinna, a determined opponent of the senate. Cinna had already opened communications with the exiled Marius and his friends, in order to compass their restoration. But Sulla could not stop to retaliate, for a dreadful massacre of Roman citizens in Asia had just been instigated by Mithradates of Pontus. Accordingly he set sail for the East, leaving behind him Appius Claudius to continue the siege of Nola, Q. Metellus Pius the son of Metellus Numidicus to act in Samnium, and Cn. Pompeius Strabo to command in Etruria.

§ **238**. Freed from the presence of Sulla and his army, Cinna took up the democratic policy where it had been left by Sulpicius. The Italians were angry at the abrogation of the law which had promised to distribute them amongst all the tribes alike: Cinna re-introduced this bill, and coupled with it another for the

Cinna and Octavius.

recall of the exiled members of Marius' party. Cn. Octavius, the senatorial champion, resisted him obstinately. Both consuls armed their followers and a pitched battle was fought in the Forum, in which Octavius prevailed and massacred 10,000 of his opponents. In defiance of all constitutional practice, Cinna was deprived of his consulate by the senate, and in his stead was elected L. Cornelius Merula (87 B.C.).

Cinna could rely upon the aid of the Italians, and he at once appealed to them. The army before Nola went over to his side; Metellus was kept inactive by the renewed assaults of the Samnites and Lucanians; Pompeius Strabo, with the army stationed in Etruria, did not appear to protect Rome until Cinna, supported by the tribune C. Papirius Carbo and by Q. Sertorius, a captain distinguished for his services in the Social War, was already encamped before the city. Here Cinna was joined by Marius, who had landed at Telamon in Etruria.

§ 239. The senate, distrustful of Strabo's loyalty, endeavoured to win over the Italians and ordered Metellus to make terms with the Samnites, but the latter were already pledged to the opposite side. Metellus then hurried to Rome with the bulk of his men to protect the senate; whereupon the Samnites and Lucanians relieved Nola, and joined Cinna in force. By this time Cn. Pompeius Strabo was dead: it was given out that he had been struck by a thunderbolt; more probably he was murdered by his mutinous soldiers. Octavius and Metellus could render no effectual aid. At last the senate, outnumbered and out-manœuvred, endeavoured to come to terms with the Marians, but the delay brought famine and pestilence into the city, and the slaves deserted to Cinna in large numbers. Ultimately the city surrendered on the

Return of Marius, 87 B.C.

mere word of Cinna that, so far as he could prevent it, there should be no bloodshed. Marius made no sign.

Cinna and Marius entered Rome, closed the gates, and for five days let loose their troops to massacre every Optimate who had not escaped. No rank was spared: Cn. Octavius and L. Merula both fell, although the latter had voluntarily resigned the consulship which had been against his will transferred to him from Cinna. There died too L. Caesar, the author of the *Lex Iulia*, and Q. Lutatius Catulus, the victor of Vercellae. Marius vented his rage like a barbarian, refusing even burial to his victims. But his career was now at an end. On Jan. 17, 86 B.C., a few days after entering upon his seventh consulship, he died.

§ **240**. Cinna named L. Valerius Flaccus consul-suffect. The former was in fact monarch, and for four years (87—84 B.C.) remained consul by his own decree, nominating even his colleagues without the pretence of election by the people. His one object was to prevent the vengeance of Sulla, whose enactments he at once declared null, forcing the senate to pronounce valid the recently renewed Sulpician law as to the distribution of the new voters; and he compelled the comitia in 86 B.C. to transfer Sulla's army to the command of L. Valerius Flaccus, who was then despatched to the East with his legate Fimbria to depose that general.

The Rule of Cinna, 87 B.C.—84 B.C.

The Italians were left to themselves and were content: the provinces mostly acquiesced in the new government, preferring anything to senatorial oppression. In 84 B.C. there arrived letters from Sulla: he had concluded peace with Mithradates, and was now on his way home with his victorious and devoted legions. The news aroused Cinna and his fellow-consul Carbo, and they planned to crush Sulla in Greece before he could reach Italy. The life of neither was safe, for Sulla's despatch declared that he was coming to put down the revolution, to restore the senatorial exiles, and to see justice done on the murderers of his friends. Cinna endeavoured to throw into Illyricum the few troops which he had still kept under arms; but they had no mind for civil war, refused to cross the sea, and tore Cinna to pieces at Ancona. It thus fell to Carbo to meet the long threatened attack.

His Death, 84 B.C.

§ 241. Before proceeding with the narration of events at Rome, we must turn back to the exploits of Sulla in the East. In 120 B.C. Mithradates VI., surnamed Eupator, succeeded on the death of his father to the kingdom of Pontus. He claimed descent from Darius Hystaspes the Persian; in bodily strength and skill he was unsurpassed; he was something of a *littérateur*; and he had bravery and subtleness to second his ambition of founding in Asia a monarchy which should oust the Romans from the East. Early in his reign he conquered the Crimea, saving from barbarians like the Roxolani of the Russian steppes the few Greek towns which still maintained their existence as the Kingdom of the Bosporus, but making them in turn his own dependencies. By the year 95 B.C. he was master of most of the north and south shores of the Black Sea, and his fleet was the most formidable in existence.

Mithradates of Pontus.

§ 242. Mithradates' first quarrel with the Romans was about the sovereignty of Cappadocia. In 96 B.C. he put a son of his own on the throne, but the senate, on the appeal of the Cappadocians, ordered a certain Ariobarzanes to be recognized as king, 93 B.C. Ariobarzanes was soon expelled by Tigranes of Armenia, at the instigation of Mithradates, but restored in 92 B.C. without difficulty by Sulla, the governor of Cilicia

The Quarrel about Cappadocia.

(which had been constituted a province since its conquest in 102 B.C.). The settlement was of no long duration. Not only was Ariobarzanes driven out a second time by Tigranes (91 B.C.), but Nicomedes III., who had just succeeded to the kingdom of Bithynia, was also attacked and dethroned. The two princes invoked the aid of Rome. M'. Aquillius, the son of that M'. Aquillius who had settled the province of Asia in 129 B.C., was sent as envoy to the East. Again there was no serious fighting. Ariobarzanes was restored to Cappadocia and Nicomedes III. to Bithynia. Not satisfied with the achievement, Aquillius, in hopes of making profit thereby, compelled the reluctant Nicomedes to declare war against Mithradates, 89 B.C. Mithradates looked for allies on all sides : to Tigranes, the powerful king of Armenia, he had already given his daughter Cleopatra ; he made overtures to the Thracians and the Greeks, intending, like Antiochus, to carry the war into Europe ; and he allied himself with the Cilician pirates. When war broke out in 88 B.C., he acted with vigour. The Bithynian king and the three Roman generals who assailed him were beaten in detail. M'. Aquillius fled to Pergamus, but was ultimately given up and tortured to death. The whole of Asia lay at the mercy of Mithradates, who met with no resistance except from Rhodes. He was hailed as a deliverer, and either in consequence of his orders or as the result of an outbreak of national fury, the Romans and Italians in Asia to the number of 80,000 were hunted down and put to death. Mithradates made Pergamus his capital, and converted Cappadocia, Phrygia, and Bithynia into satrapies. By his powerful fleet which swept the Aegean, he was able to send his generals across to Greece and to raise the whole peninsula against Rome, 87 B.C. Sparta, Achaea, and Boeotia were willing to help ;

The First Mithradatic War, 88 B.C.—84 B.C.

and Athens opened its gates to the Pontic admiral Archelaus. At the same time more Pontic troops were sent into Greece by way of Macedonia.

§ **243**. By this time Sulla had landed in Epirus with 30,000 men. He knew that his leaving Rome at this moment meant the overthrow of his recent measures and the triumph of Cinna and Marius; but not to leave Rome meant the loss of the Eastern Empire. His first move was to offer Mithradates terms of peace, by which the Great King might retire on giving up his recent acquisitions. When the offer was declined Sulla marched upon Athens, and having defeated Archelaus in Boeotia, proceeded to invest the city. Such rapid successes speedily influenced the cowardly Greeks: most of the towns bought pardon by instant submission and by gifts of men, money, or supplies. Archelaus and his coadjutor Aristion defended Athens and its harbour the Piraeus for many months. Assault was useless, and the slow method of blockade alone could be employed; but even this was a difficulty while Mithradates commanded the seas and supplied the city from his vast resources.

Sulla in Greece.

It was not until March 1st, 86 B.C., that Athens capitulated. It was plundered of course, but not deprived of its freedom. Mithradates grew impatient. He might have ruined Sulla's army by a policy of delay: he chose rather to push matters to a head. His general Taxiles, who was in Macedonia with 100,000 foot, marched into Greece. In Boeotia he was joined by the forces which Archelaus now withdrew from the Piraeus; and the two generals gave battle to Sulla at Chaeronea (*Kaprena*) in March, 86 B.C. They were utterly defeated, and only a miserable remnant under Archelaus escaped to Chalcis.

Capture of Athens, 86 B.C.

Battle of Chaeronea, 86 B.C.

§ **244.** In spite of this brilliant victory Sulla was still unable to move. He had no fleet, and the utmost endeavours of his legate L. Licinius Lucullus could not collect one; and at this very moment the Cinnan consul, L. Valerius Flaccus (§ 240), was in Epirus, invested by his party with the task of disarming Sulla rather than of crushing Mithradates. But Flaccus was incapable; finding that his men were more likely to desert to Sulla than Sulla's to come over to himself, he avoided a battle, and passed into Macedonia, intending to enter Asia by way of the Hellespont and attack Mithradates at home.

L. Valerius Flaccus in Greece.

In the same or the following year (86 or 85 B.C.), the Great King sent another expedition into Greece. Archelaus, still with the chief command, again massed his forces in Boeotia, only to fight a second battle with no better result than before. So completely was he defeated at Orchomenus (*Skripu*), that he lost even his camp and barely escaped to Euboea (*Negropont*). As a result, the Pontic forces practically evacuated Europe, and Sulla, after some futile negotiations with Archelaus, spent the ensuing winter in preparing to invade Asia.

Battle of Orchomenus, 85 B.C.

The consul Flaccus, escaping from Sulla, had crossed the Hellespont and reached Chalcedon in Asia when a mutiny broke out in which he lost his life. It was headed by a demagogue of no birth, C. Flavius Fimbria, who now took up the command and defeated a Pontic army on the Rhyndacus. At the same time L. Lucullus appeared with a small but well-handled fleet raised from Rhodes and other island states. Fimbria invited his co-operation to capture Mithradates in Mitylene, but Lucullus was too loyal a Sullan, and went on with his own business

Death of Flaccus.

of recovering in detail the islands and maritime towns. After this he met Sulla in Thrace, and conveyed the troops of the latter across to the Troad, 84 B.C.

§ **245.** The conduct of Mithradates had already alienated the Asiatics: he murdered, confiscated, and insulted on all hands, robbing the rich to find gifts for his favourites and extorting money for the war by every possible means. *End of the First Mithradatic War.* The various cities showed their resentment by welcoming Lucullus, and the Great King saw fit to offer terms. He endeavoured to purchase his conquests in Asia by offering to support Sulla against the Mario-Cinnan democracy. Sulla refused to surrender any portion of Roman Asia, demanded the complete restoration of the king's recent conquests, a war-indemnity of 3000 talents and the surrender of Archelaus' fleet. Mithradates at last accepted the terms, and then Sulla turned to settle accounts with Fimbria. It was easily done, for Sulla's forces were far the more numerous, and Fimbria's men began to desert at once. The self-made general fled to Pergamus and there killed himself. His two legions took service with Sulla, and were placed under the command of L. Licinius Murena, an officer who had done good service at the siege of Athens and elsewhere.

The organization of the recovered provinces was rapid and thorough. Nicomedes III. and Ariobarzanes were reseated upon the thrones of Bithynia and *Settlement of Asia.* Cappadocia, and Mithradates bound himself to live peaceably with them. The few states and towns which had been loyal to Rome—Rhodes, Chios, Magnesia, etc.—were rewarded by the grant of new lands or further privileges. Those which had rebelled were reduced to the *status quo ante*, and were called upon for the tribute which they had neglected to pay during the past five years. The men who had taken a prominent part in the massacre of the Italians were executed. A war-indemnity of 20,000 talents was levied. Sulla had recovered the Eastern Empire, but the cost of the war left its mark upon the provincials, for they now fell more deeply still into the toils of the Roman usurers, toils from which they never escaped until the Republic was overthrown.

§ 246. L. Licinius Murena, left by Sulla in command of the province, was determined to force on a second war with Mithradates. Making a pretext of some preparations of the Pontic king against the revolted Bosporians, he began to plunder the territories of Mithradates. The latter appealed to the senate at Rome, but Murena seems to have been encouraged by that body to continue the war. On the river Halys however he was defeated with great loss, and compelled to retreat into Phrygia. Soon afterwards there came peremptory orders from Sulla that he should desist from hostilities. Murena obeyed, and for some years Mithradates and the Romans were on good terms with each other.

Second Mithradatic War, 83 B.C.—82 B.C.

§ 247. The consuls for 83 B.C., the year in which Sulla sailed home from Greece, were C. Norbanus and L. Cornelius Scipio Asiaticus, the latter a descendant of the victor of Magnesia. Neither was a general: nevertheless they got under arms upwards of 150,000 men to oppose the bare 30,000 of Sulla. The Italians as a whole sided with the government, for the success of Sulla meant the restoration of the senate, and perhaps, as they dreaded, their own disenfranchisement. Most of all the Samnites and Lucanians flocked to resist his return. Landing at Brundisium, Sulla overran Apulia without hindrance. Here he was joined by many of the exiled nobles: chief among these were Q. Metellus Pius

Sulla returns to Italy, 83 B.C.

and the famous Gnaeus Pompeius, of whom the latter, son of Cn. Pompeius Strabo, had declared for Sulla in Picenum, where he had many clients, and had raised a force of three legions. In Campania Norbanus barred the way, and Sulla, finding negotiations again fruitless, attacked and utterly routed him in the battle of Mount Tifata. Hurrying thence northward he met Scipio at Teanum (*Teano*) and proposed a conference. The two leaders arrived at no decision; but Sulla's veterans, mixing with the recruits of Scipio, persuaded them to desert their commander, and the second consular army thus fell before the invader.

§ **248**. In 82 B.C. the revolutionists made a desperate effort to recover their lost ground. Carbo and C. Marius, the adopted son of **the great Marius**, were consuls: the former held this office now for the third time; the latter was invested with it at the age of twenty-six, for it was hoped that, for his father's sake, men would hasten to serve under the son's standards. Sulla, after wintering in Campania, advanced into Latium, and at Sacriportus near Signia (*Segni*) met and defeated Marius, and shut up the remnant of his army in Praeneste (*Palestrina*), entrusting the siege of that strong fortress to Ofella. By the orders of Marius, Brutus Damasippus the praetor evacuated Rome, but not before he had convoked the senate in the Curia and there cut down the few adherents of Sulla who had survived thus far. A few hours later Sulla entered the capital, placed in it a garrison, and hurried on towards Etruria, where Carbo held at bay the second division of the Sullan forces under Metellus Pius. This officer had captured several scattered divisions, stormed Sena Gallica (*Sinigaglia*), and by the help of Pompeius had driven Carbo back upon Ariminum (*Rimini*). Carbo now moved into Etruria, and there the Sullans beset him on all

The Campaign of 82 B.C.

sides. His first engagement was with Sulla in person at Clusium (*Chiusi*), and proved so favourable to Carbo that he detached a large column to relieve the siege of Praeneste. At the same time the entire body of the Samnites and Lucanians, 70,000 men under Pontius of Telesia and M. Lamponius, raised the siege of Capua and advanced to the relief of Praeneste. Carbo's column was cut to pieces at Spoletium (*Spoleto*), and Sulla returned in person to face the Samnites. About the same time C. Norbanus, after some successes in Gallia Cisalpina, was defeated and forced to fly to Rhodes. The victorious Sullans, under Lucullus and Metellus, moved upon Carbo, who gave up hope and fled to Africa. The repeated attempts to save Praeneste had failed. The forces of Ofella blockaded the doomed fortress as vigorously as ever, and the revolutionists in despair resolved to signalize their own destruction by the sack of Rome. The Samnites especially lusted to rase "the wolves' den," and on November 1st, 82 B.C., their entire host quitted the neighbourhood of Praeneste and encamped before the Colline Gate. Sulla hastened to save the city. He appeared within a few hours, and despite the exhaustion of his men, gave battle forthwith. The fight lasted twenty-four hours and left Sulla barely victorious. Rome was saved; the army of the Revolution was destroyed. C. Marius committed suicide and Praeneste surrendered, only to be sacked. One by one the few remaining towns fell. Nola, garrisoned by Mutilus and his Samnites, held out until 80 B.C., and Volaterrae in Etruria did not submit until 79 B.C.

Battle of the Colline Gate, 82 B.C.

§ **249.** Italy and the East were thus in the hands of Sulla; but Sicily, Spain, and Africa were held by scattered bands of Cinna's adherents. Q. Sertorius escaping from Etruria raised a force in Spain, but

The Sullans in the West.

§ 250.] DICTATORSHIP OF SULLA. 333

was soon forced to fly, though, as we shall see, he afterwards returned and defied the Sullans for many years. M. Perpenna withdrew from Sicily at the mere approach of Pompeius, who soon afterwards captured Carbo and put him to death (80 B.C.). Crossing thence to Africa, Pompeius found himself opposed by a large army under Cn. Domitius Ahenobarbus. He finished the war within forty days. When he was recalled and ordered to disband his army, his men claimed for him a triumph which Sulla saw fit to accord, though **Pompeius was not yet of senatorial rank** (79 B.C.).

§ **250.** The battle of the Colline Gate left Sulla undisputed master of Rome, and free to take what vengeance he pleased on his enemies. Three successive lists of proscribed persons were drawn up, until nearly five thousand men of note were marked out as fit objects for any one to kill; and many more died because their wealth tempted the greed of Sulla's satellites. Their goods and lands were given away or auctioned by Sulla—he called them his spoils—at prices that were almost nominal. By a law of unprecedented injustice, the children and grandchildren of the proscribed were forbidden ever to hold office. All Italy suffered as did Rome. Throughout Etruria there were wholesale massacres; in Samnium scarcely a single town except Beneventum remained standing; flourishing communities like Norba, Praeneste, Interamna, and Florentia were spoiled and deprived of their charters because they had the misfortune to be on the losing side. On the lands thus acquired Sulla settled 120,000 of his legionaries, on whose loyalty he knew he might rely should any resistance to his despotism be offered. But resistance there was none. Towards the close of 82 B.C., both consuls being now dead, the senate nominated as

Sulla's Reign of Terror, 82 B.C.

interrex L. Valerius Flaccus, the cousin of that Flaccus who was cut off by the mutineer Fimbria. To Flaccus Sulla addressed a despatch: the disorders of the state were such, he declared, as to require one man's hand to heal them; a perpetual dictator was the desideratum, and he offered his services. There could be no refusal: and in 81 B.C. Sulla assumed the dictatorship, which being limited neither in time nor place, resembled rather a Greek Tyrannis than the old republican magistracy last held by Fabius Cunctator.

§ **251.** Throughout 81 B.C. and the following year Sulla was busy in re-fashioning the constitution. His main and indeed sole object was to place the authority of the senate on a secure and legal basis, so that it should have nothing to fear from the popular assemblies on the one hand, or from powerful magistrates on the other. The senate, depleted by the recent wars and proscriptions, was filled up by three hundred new members, elected in theory by the tribes, but really of the dictator's own choosing. A series of laws now gave it the supreme power in the state, for (1) the tribunician office, that had proved so irresistible in the hands of the Gracchi and their successors, was degraded by various restrictions, and the tribune was forbidden to lay measures before the assemblies; (2) the Comitia Centuriata was to replace the Comitia Tributa as the great popular body for the making of laws, and no bill was to be laid before it which had not previously received the assent of the senate (*senatus auctoritas*); and (3) the Equestrian Order was deprived of its right to send jurors to the standing commissions.

The Leges Corneliae, 81 B.C.

The Senate.

§ **252.** Considerable changes were made in the position of the magistrates. The tribunate suffered severely, for it was deprived of most of the powers which had accrued to it in the course of time. The tribune could still protect a citizen by his right of veto; but he could neither check a decree of the senate, nor stop a vote of the assembly, nor throw a magistrate into prison. Most important of all, he was absolutely debarred from proposing a law to the assembly. There were personal restrictions also attached to the office: probably no one but a senator could be elected, and the very holding of the tribunate was made a bar to any higher magistracy. To meet the requirements of the provinces, now ten in number,[1] the six praetors were increased to eight, and the eight quaestors to twenty.[2] Consuls and praetors were no longer sent to govern the provinces in their year of office. During that period they remained in Rome to superintend the civil and legal business of the city: the consuls had a general power of control; of the praetors, the *praetor urbanus* and the *praetor peregrinus* retained their old functions, while the remaining six sat as presidents in the newly-established *quaestiones perpetuae* (§ 253). On the expiration of their year of office, the two consuls and the eight praetors were, as proconsuls and propraetors respectively, sent abroad to govern the ten provinces. The result of this was that the civil and military authority were no longer in the same hands, and so the magistrate was less formidable to the senate. The quaestorship henceforth entitled a man to a seat in the

The Magistrates.

---

[1] Sicily, Sardinia and Corsica, the two Spains, Macedonia, Africa, Asia, Gallia Narbonensis, Cilicia, and Gallia Cisalpina (constituted a province by Sulla).

[2] The quaestors were apportioned as follows two (*quaestores urbani*) were treasury officials at Rome; two (*quaestores militares*) acted as paymasters to the troops on service; four (*quaestores classici*) attended to the fleet, eleven (two in Sicily and one in each of the remaining nine provinces) supervised the finances of the provinces; the duties of the twentieth are not known; cp. § 191.

senate, and as there were now twenty quaestors, there was no need of a censor for the purpose of filling up vacancies. Accordingly the censorship fell for a time into abeyance, and no censor was appointed for twelve years. To further check any usurpation on the part of the magistrates, two laws were revived: (1) no magistrate was to be eligible a second time to a curule office until ten years had elapsed since his first tenure of such office; (2) no one was to be consul before being quaestor and praetor, and the earliest age at which the quaestorship, praetorship, and consulship could be attained was fixed respectively at 30, 40, and 43.

§ **253**. The power of the people was limited by the Comitia Centuriata taking the place of the Comitia Tributa as the organ for making laws. Another change tending to the same end was the repeal of the *Lex Domitia* of 104 B.C. which had committed the election of Pontiffs and Augurs to the votes of seventeen tribes, chosen from the whole thirty-five by lot: Sulla now reverted to the old system, by which the members of the priestly colleges filled up vacancies by co-optation. A more defensible piece of legislation was the abolition of the cornlargesses instituted by C. Gracchus.

The People.

The Equites suffered an equal loss of position. Sulla increased the standing commissions (*quaestiones perpetuae*) to the number of nine. Besides the court for trying cases of extortion (*quaestio de repetundis*), established by the *Lex Calpurnia* of 149 B.C., there were now courts for treason (*maiestatis*), violence (*de vi*), assassination (*de sicariis*), parricide (*de parricidio*), poisoning (*de veneficiis*), forgery (*de falso*), and other offences. The six praetors acted as presidents, and the jurors were no longer taken exclusively or even in part from the Equestrian

The Iudicia.

§ 254.]   WEAKNESS OF HIS LEGISLATION.   337

Order. By Sulla's arrangement, senators alone were capable of serving.

§ 254. Such a constitution, fraught as it was with the seeds of discontent and hatred, could only be permanent if the governing class which it benefited was capable and honest. But the nobility was weaker now than it had ever been, for proscriptions and wars had robbed it of even the poor support of a conservatism founded upon tradition : it was a nobility of parvenus. Almost every other class in the state resented the treatment it had received from Sulla : the proletariate demanded the re-establishment of the corn-doles ; the democrats agitated for the restoration of the tribunician authority ; the Equites desired to recover control of the law-courts. Outside Rome the Italians were alienated by the massacres at Praeneste and elsewhere, and by the confiscation of their lands for the benefit of Sulla's veterans ; the soldiery who occupied their farms knew nothing of agriculture, so that wide tracts of country ran to waste, while the *latifundia* increased and the free population almost disappeared. Last of all there was growing up a class of men who had lost or made fortunes in previous revolutions, and looked to new seditions as the speediest way of enriching themselves.

Weak points of Sulla's legislation.

CHAPTER X.

THE FIRST AND SECOND TRIUMVIRATES.

§§ 255, 256. The Rising of Lepidus.—§§ 257, 258. Sertorius.—
§ 259. The War of Spartacus.—§ 260. The First Consulship of
Pompeius and Crassus.—§§ 261—268. The Third Mithradatic War.
—§ 269. Cicero.—§ 270. Caesar.—§§ 271—280. The Conspiracies of
Catilina to the Murder of Clodius.—§ 281. The Parthian War.—
§§ 282—290. Caesar in Gaul.—§§ 291—295. Struggle between
Caesar and the Senate.—§§ 296—299. Constitutional Measures and
Death of Caesar.—§§ 300—310. History of the Second Triumvirate.

§ **255.** In 79 B.C. Sulla laid down the dictatorship and
retired to the privacy of his villa at Cumae,
where he died in the following spring, 78 B.C.
The consuls for 78 B.C. were Q. Lutatius Catulus, son of
the conqueror of Vercellae, and M. Aemilius Lepidus. The
latter had been threatened with impeachment for extortion
in Sicily, and to avoid condemnation he suddenly deserted
the senatorial party and ranged himself with the democrats.
Scarcely was Sulla dead when Lepidus, encouraged by the
recent successes of Sertorius in Spain, made an assault on
the new constitution. First and foremost, the tribunate
was to be re-established and the corn-doles renewed.
After this, all lands and property confiscated during the
recent dictatorship were to be restored, and the sentences
by which the adherents of Cinna had been banished, and
their children debarred from public office, were to be
rescinded. The senate, growing alarmed, made a half-

The Rising of Lepidus.

hearted attempt at a compromise: the corn-doles were renewed on the original plan of C. Gracchus, but only in favour of a limited number of the citizens. But the discontented did not wait for the sanction of law: the evicted people of Faesulae in Etruria proceeded to oust the Sullan allotment-holders, and the disputes which followed soon gave the senate opportunity to declare the state in danger, and to despatch Lepidus and Catulus to the disturbed districts. This foolish proceeding would inevitably furnish the head of the sedition with troops; but the senate hoped to keep Lepidus quiet by administering to him an oath not to turn his arms against his colleague. The consul took the oath, remarking that it would only bind him during his year of office, and went on raising fresh troops for the revolution. He refused to return when recalled, and at the beginning of 77 B.C. sent to demand the restoration of the exiles and the tribunate, and a second consulship for himself.

§ **256.** These demands were refused, and Lepidus marched upon Rome. The capital was protected by Catulus and the Sullan veterans, to whom a revolution meant the loss of all their recent gains. Cn. Pompeius was despatched to Cisalpine Gaul, where M. Brutus, legate of Lepidus, was at the head of a small force. In a battle fought on the Campus Martius, under the very walls of Rome, Lepidus was defeated and withdrew to Etruria. His legate Brutus was still less successful: he was besieged by Pompeius in Mutina (*Modena*), captured, and put to death. Lepidus contrived to take ship from Etruria after a second engagement, and sailed to Sardinia, where he hoped to maintain himself by the aid of Sertorius. He died, however, before he could effect anything; and Perpenna, the Cinnan leader who had abandoned Sicily to

Defeat of Lepidus, 77 B.C.

Pompeius (§ 249), carried the remnant of Lepidus' men into Spain.

§ **257.** In 80 B.C. Q. Sertorius, who had previously withdrawn from Spain, returned thither on the invitation of the Lusitanians. Though he had comparatively few troops, he completely succeeded in his attacks on the Sullan generals who were sent against him. The most formidable of these, Q. Metellus Pius, he routed on the Anas (*Guadiana*), while his lieutenant Hirtuleius was as fortunate in the Hither province. Continuing to act with great skill, Sertorius was by 77 B.C. in possession of the entire peninsula, except a few coast towns. From the exiled Marians who flocked to him for protection he formed a senate and found officers for his Spanish army. His chivalry of character gained the affection of the Spaniards, whom he protected against the insolence of his Roman troops, and refused to oppress by excessive tribute, while he worked on their superstition by pretending to be a favourite of Diana, and to receive instructions from her through the agency of a tame fawn. In 77 B.C. he was joined by M. Perpenna with the remnant of Lepidus' army.

Sertorius in Spain.

§ **258.** At this juncture Cn. Pompeius arrived to carry on the war. He was fresh from his victory over M. Brutus, on the strength of which he had demanded the post of general in Spain. The senate would gladly have refused; but Pompeius declined to disband his forces, and to avert worse things the senate gave way and invested Pompeius with proconsular authority in Spain. He reached that country in 76 B.C., after passing through Gaul, and at once marched southwards to join Metellus in the Further province. He forced the passage of the Iberus (*Ebro*) in the face of Perpenna,

Murder of Sertorius, 72 B.C.

but was out-generalled by Sertorius in the rest of the campaign. The year 75 B.C. saw the defeat and death at Segovia of Hirtuleius, an irreparable misfortune for Sertorius, which was followed by the junction of Metellus and Pompeius. By the end of the year the senatorial generals were in complete possession of Further Spain, and the war now centred about the Ebro valley and the important towns of Ilerda (*Lerida*), Calagurris (*Calahorra*) and Osca (*Huesca*). Here Sertorius still held his ground. There were few battles, many sieges; and each winter Metellus and Pompeius, owing to lack of supplies, were compelled to retire, one into Southern Spain, the other beyond the Pyrenees. At last Sertorius fell. It was said that he had forgotten his early frankness and simple habits: at any rate he could no longer rely upon the Spaniards, and his own intimate friends conspired to murder him. Twice they failed, and many of them paid with their lives for their treachery. Perpenna, however, consummated this villainy by assassinating his general at a banquet at Osca. He had hoped to obtain the place of the murdered leader, but men had no confidence in him, and when he fell into Pompeius' hands he was ordered off to execution. So ended the Sertorian War. 72 B.C.

§ 259. When Pompeius returned to Italy, he found the land devastated by a slave war. Not only were the agrarian evils, which Tiberius Gracchus had tried to combat, more rampant than ever, but the growing popularity of gladiatorial shows had led to the establishment of regular schools (*ludi*) for training the most desperate class of slaves—condemned criminals, prisoners of war, and the like—for their appearance in the arena. It was natural that these men should use the skill so acquired to preserve their lives, and in 73 B.C. a

The War of Spartacus, 73—71 B.C.

band of seventy picked gladiators, headed by Spartacus, a Thracian of noble blood, and by Crixus and Oenomaus, two Celtic prisoners, broke out of a training school at Capua and escaped to Mount Vesuvius. The insurgents, increased by numbers of runaway slaves from all parts, defeated the magistrates sent against them, and soon all Southern Italy was at the mercy of Spartacus and 40,000 savages, who stormed and sacked the old Greek towns of the coast. So formidable was the war, that in 72 B.C. both consuls took the field. Crixus, who had quarrelled with Spartacus, was defeated and killed in Apulia; but this loss was forgotten in a series of victories which Spartacus won soon afterwards. He defeated both consuls and traversed Italy from end to end, even appearing as far north as Mutina. To wipe out this disgrace, the consuls were in the autumn superseded by M. Licinius Crassus, the richest man in Rome and the representative of the Equites. Spartacus retreated into Bruttium with the design of crossing to Sicily; but the pirates upon whom he relied to carry him across the straits, played him false. Turning northwards again he broke through the lines which Crassus had constructed across Bruttium from sea to sea, but dissensions once more broke out among his followers, of whom the entire German and Celtic portion seceded. 71 B.C. They were cut off by Crassus to the last man, and Spartacus himself soon afterwards perished in a great battle in Lucania. The survivors were hunted down by Pompeius, who had by this time finished the Sertorian War and was marching to the support of Crassus.

§ **260**. Thus far the Sullan constitution had endured: the repeated attacks of the democrats had only resulted in the re-establishment of the corn-largess and the removal of the restriction which had made a tribune ineligible for other offices. But the discontent was great among all classes: the popular party clamoured for the restoration of the tribunate to its old dignity, the Equites demanded that they should again serve in the jury-courts, while both declaimed against the corruption of the senatorial jurymen and governors, of whom the notorious Verres was about this time being impeached for hideous oppression and cruelty in Sicily. When therefore in 71 B.C. Pompeius and Crassus returned to Rome, each bringing with him a victorious army, the senate looked on with unconcealed dread, while its opponents were filled with hope. The generals did not disappoint the popular expectation. On being elected to the consulship for 70 B.C., they led the attack on the government, keeping their armies close to the city in case of need. There were passed three great bills—

The First Consulship of Pompeius and Crassus, 70 B.C.

(i) That the tribunes should again be allowed to bring measures before the assembly.
(ii) That the jury-courts (*iudicia*) should be divided between one decuria of senators and two of Equites.
(iii) That the censorship should be restored with its old power over the senate.

The whole of Sulla's work was undone, except that his reforms concerning the jurisdiction of the standing commissions (*quaestiones perpetuae*) and the division of magisterial duties remained untouched. The tribunician power again became as threatening to the government as it had ever been, and the censors appointed in accordance with the new legislation ejected no fewer than sixty-four members from the senate. Before their year of office was over Pompeius and Crassus quarrelled, and seemed about to turn their armies against each other, but the democrats brought about a half-hearted reconciliation. The consuls disbanded their legions and became private citizens again. Pompeius however was eager to win fresh laurels, and looked anxiously to the east for the chance of doing so.

§ 261. Since his defeat by Sulla, Mithradates had regained much of his old power. For allies he had the Cilician pirates by sea and Armenia by land; and inasmuch as Rome had destroyed all the other Mediterranean fleets without adequately arming one of her own, the pirates were, if properly handled, invincible, and might even prevent the appearance of any Roman forces in Asia; while Tigranes of Armenia, son-in-law of Mithradates, had almost immediately upon Sulla's retirement from Asia, commenced a series of aggressions which had added a great part of Mesopotamia, Cappadocia and Syria to his dominions, and broken to pieces the empire of the Seleucidae. His boundaries were on the east the Caspian Sea, on the north the kingdom of Mithradates and the Caucasus, on the south the Parthians, whom he had reduced to comparative helplessness. On the west his limit was where he might choose to set it, and Mithradates wished him to swoop at once upon Roman Asia.

Mithradates of Pontus.

§ 262. Dying in 75 B.C., Nicomedes III. left his kingdom of Bithynia to the Romans. This meant the extension of Roman Asia to the very borders of Pontus, and Mithradates knew that sooner or later it would lead to a collision between himself and Rome. He promptly overran Bithynia, made overtures of alliance to Sertorius, and obtained from him a number of exiled Romans to drill his army of 100,000 men and to act as his officers. The pirates assisted in providing him with a fleet of 400 vessels.

Bithynia is bequeathed to Rome, 75 B.C.

The consuls for 74 B.C. were L. Licinius Lucullus and M. Aurelius Cotta. Lucullus, who had been one of Sulla's most capable officers in the First Mithradatic War, was a staunch optimate, but fonder of ease than of politics; and he was that rare citizen, an honest man, who would wink neither at equestrian oppressions nor at military excesses. **Supported by Cotta** as his admiral on the Hellespont, he commenced the attack by marching through Phrygia with a force of 30,000 men. Luckily for him, Tigranes left Mithradates to take care of himself, but even thus the Romans were seriously out-numbered. By this time Mithradates had got as far as Calchedon (*Kadikoï*), where he was besieging Cotta. He burnt the Roman fleet in the harbour, but learning that Lucullus was coming to the rescue, he passed on to Cyzicus (*Balkiz*). There he found himself entrapped, unable either to advance or retreat, while want of supplies bred sickness amongst his host (74 B.C.). He was at length compelled, after losing two-thirds of his infantry and almost all his cavalry, to put the residue on board his fleet. Further disasters occurred at sea, and only a stroke of good fortune enabled him to reach Pontus upon a pirate vessel, 73 B.C.

<small>The Third Mithradatic War, 74— 65 B.C.</small>

§ **263**. The Romans now assumed the aggressive, and in the following year, 72 B.C., Lucullus surprised the Pontic army at Cabira (*Niksar*), and forced Mithradates to take refuge with Tigranes of Armenia. Then leaving his legates to reduce the coast towns, he returned to re-organize the province of Asia. The reduction of the coast was not accomplished for two years, and the re-organization of Asia was attended with difficulties almost as tedious, for the land was brought to the verge of ruin by the exactions of Roman tax-gatherers and money-lenders, following upon the exhausting wars of Sulla. Lucullus performed his task well from the provincials' point of view, less well from his own; for his rectitude raised up against him the enmity of the entire

<small>Battle of Cabira, 72 B.C.</small>

Equestrian order, and though they could not avenge themselves at once, they found means to do so later on.

§ 264. It was evident to Lucullus that Asia could not be secure while Tigranes was unchastised, yet he knew that the inert home-government would never authorize him to attack so formidable a power as Armenia. But he was determined to act, and in order to find a valid excuse for war, he sent to Tigranes envoys demanding the surrender of Mithradates. Tigranes was astounded at such a message from a general whose entire force was under 30,000 men: he gave an emphatic refusal, which was all Lucullus desired, and before the Armenian army could be collected a Roman force of 15,000 men had laid siege to Tigranocerta, a new city which Tigranes had peopled with Greek captives from Cappadocia and Syria. In attempting to relieve the town Tigranes was defeated utterly: he lost, said Lucullus' despatch, 100,000 men as against five Romans slain, and the town itself was surrendered (69 B.C.).

Lucullus attacks Tigranes.

Battle of Tigranocerta, 69 B.C.

§ 265. Yet Mithradates was able to induce the Armenians to continue the struggle, though he failed to find an ally in Phraates of Parthia, who made a treaty on his own account with Rome. Accordingly in the following spring, Lucullus marched eastward into Armenia Proper, intending to attack Artaxata (*Ardaschar*), the capital of the empire. But the country was difficult, the weather severe, the soldiers weary of long service and of the sternness with which their general prevented them from plundering while he made a fortune for himself. They mutinied, and compelled him to march back across the Tigris, and his only exploit in this year (68 B.C.) was the sack of Nisibis. But meanwhile Mithradates had armed new forces, and successfully assailed the weak detachments

Reverses of Lucullus.

which Lucullus had left behind him in Pontus. His legates sent urgent demands for help, and Lucullus reluctantly abandoned Nisibis, Tigranocerta, and all his recent conquests, 67 B.C. Even so he arrived too late: the Romans had already sustained a severe defeat at Zela (*Zilleh*), and news now arrived from Rome that the people, instigated by the Equites, had deprived Lucullus of the command, and superseded him by the consul M'. Acilius Glabrio. Fresh mutinies broke out among his troops: he could not induce them to confront Mithradates, who overran Cappadocia without hindrance, and he had the mortification to see once more in the possession of the enemy every inch of ground that he had conquered in his eight campaigns. After witnessing this melancholy issue of his brilliant exploits he retired into private life, and spent his days in luxury and literary pursuits, leaving a name that was to be proverbial for wealthy refinement and indolence.

§ 266. The pirates had deserted Mithradates in his hour of defeat, but only to resume the more profitable employment of piracy in the western seas, and to make life a burden to the coast towns and merchants of Italy. Again all classes in Rome clamoured for deliverance from the corsairs, and turned to Pompeius for help, although the democrats were almost as much afraid as was the senate that he might ultimately prove another Sulla or Marius.

The Gabinian Law, 67 B.C.

Accordingly the tribune Aulus Gabinius brought in a bill conferring upon Pompeius the conduct of the war against the pirates, with proconsular power for three years over the entire Mediterranean and the whole coast to a distance of fifty miles inland. He was to have twenty-five legates of his own choosing, and whatever supplies and funds he desired. Such a bill showed that the fall of the

Republic was very near, for it set up a private citizen as virtual monarch. **The bill was carried, and** at once the starvation prices which had until then ruled in the markets dropped to the normal rate. Pompeius raised a fleet, swept the western seas, drove the pirates before him to Cilicia, and there **routed their** united squadrons in a final battle off Coracesium. The whole war was begun and ended in ninety days, and the general might again have sunk into privacy but for the conduct of another tribune, C. Manilius, who proposed that, as Pompeius was now in Asia, he should receive the command in the war with Mithradates. The powers conferred by the *Lex Gabinia* were not superseded; they were merely extended until such time as Pompeius should choose to declare the war ended. He was left entirely at liberty to make war or peace. There was little opposition, for the senate had learnt its weakness. Q. Catulus, now an old man, endeavoured, as in the case of the Gabinian law, to prevent the passing of a bill so fatal to Republican ideas.

<small>The Manilian Law, 66 B.C.</small>

§ **267**. In 66 B.C. Pompeius landed in Cilicia, and under the provisions of the *Lex Manilia*, took the command against Mithradates. Men said that he only came to reap the results of Lucullus' labours; but by this time Mithradates had recovered his kingdom, and the war had to be begun afresh. After much manœuvring, Pompeius crossed the Pontic border, and, where afterwards he built the city of Nicopolis (near *Enderes*), entrapped the enemy in a ravine and cut his entire host to pieces (66 B.C.). Mithradates, again a fugitive, and now disowned by Tigranes, fled beyond the Caucasus to Panticapaeum (*Kertch*), the capital of that principality of the Russian Chersonese (*Crimea*) over which his rebel son Machares was suzerain. For a moment

<small>Pompeius defeats Mithradates.</small>

Pompeius seemed disposed to follow, but the hostility of the Caucasian tribes, and the impassable nature of the country, caused him to alter his purpose; and after traversing Armenia as far as Artaxata, receiving the abject submission of Tigranes, and chastising the Iberians and Albanians (65 B.C.), he withdrew beyond the Euphrates to Syria (64 B.C.), and proceeded to settle the affairs of what was once the empire of the Seleucidae. Mithradates, still indomitable, set himself to equip and drill yet another army: it was said that he intended rousing against Rome the warlike tribes of Thrace and the Danube valley. But the patience of his people was exhausted by his levies and his exactions for fresh war-material; his son Pharnaces joined in their revolt, and disaffection spread so rapidly that Mithradates was unable even to fly, and slew himself to save from parricide the son who now sent to Pompeius news of his exploit and assurance of his loyalty (63 B.C.). *End of Mithradates, 63 B.C.*

§ 268. In the settlement of Asia, the new frontier was, roughly speaking, to be the rivers Halys and Euphrates: Bithynia, with the western half of Pontus, was constituted a province, as was also Syria (the kingdom of Seleucus) as far as the frontiers of Judaea; Cilicia was rearranged so as to include Pamphylia, Pisidia, and part of Cappadocia. Ariobarzanes I. was restored to the throne of Cappadocia, and Deiotarus received most of Galatia. The Jews, who had under the rule of the Maccabees become a formidable power, were constrained to accept as king the high priest John Hyrcanus, who had for years been disputing the throne with his brother Aristobulus. When Pompeius returned to Rome he left behind him peace in lieu of anarchy, and a frontier whose only menace was the power of Parthia; and *Settlement of Asia by Pompeius.*

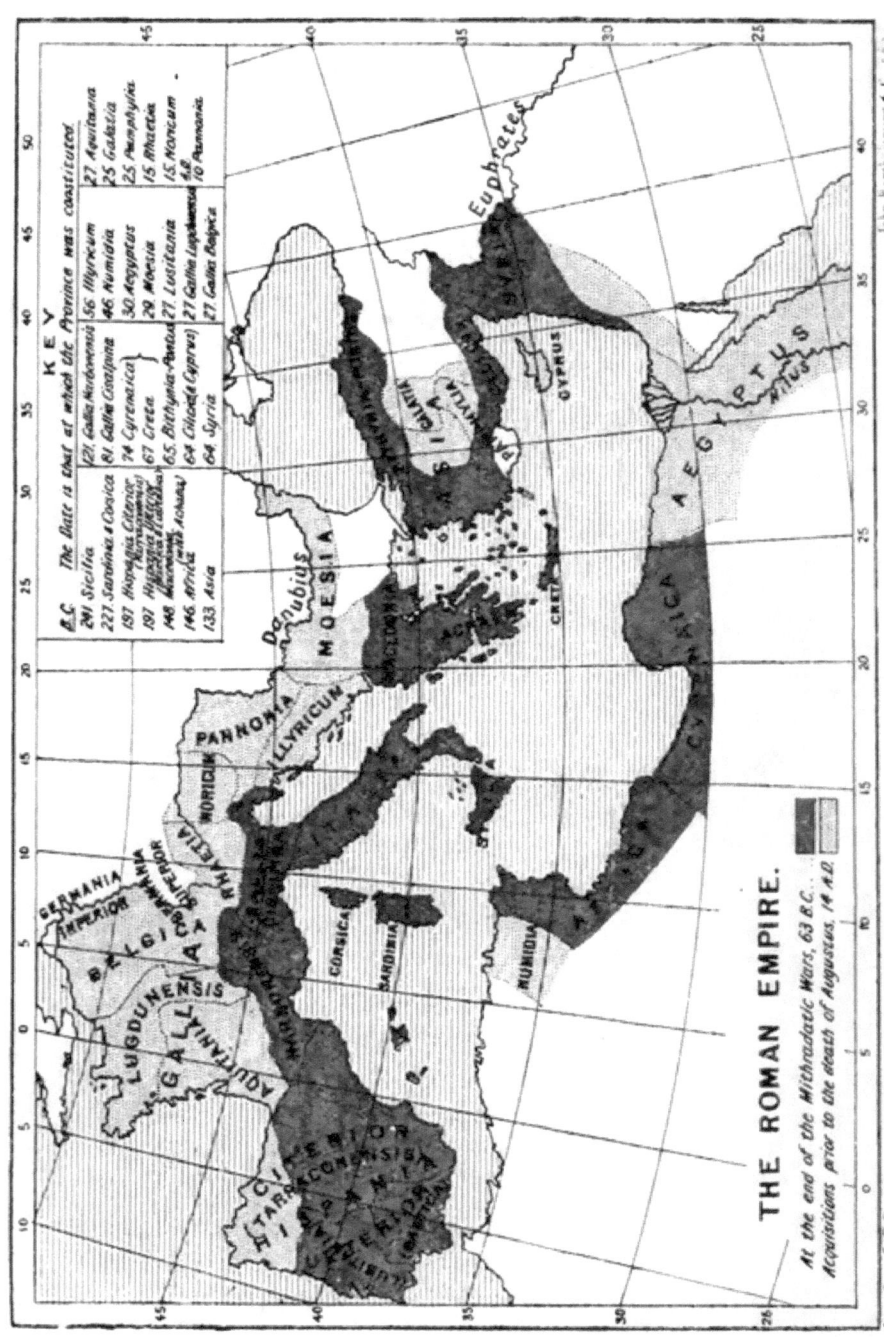

he paid into the treasury two hundred millions of sesterces, reserving twice that amount as largess and prize-money for the troops with whom, barely 40,000 men, he claimed to have conquered twelve millions of Orientals—with whom he had certainly humbled the great empires of Western Asia.

§ 269. While Pompeius was absent in the East, two men at Rome had risen into prominence. These were Cicero and Caesar. M. Tullius Cicero, the son of a knight of Arpinum, began his career by pleading in the law-courts, as was customary with young men who aimed at political distinction. His bold defence of Sextus Roscius of Ameria against a worthless favourite of Sulla, attracted public notice, and even aroused the resentment of the dictator. After travelling for two years in Greece and Asia, Cicero renewed his forensic labours at Rome. His success was conspicuous, and he obtained the quaestorship in 75 B.C. In his year of office, which was spent in Sicily, he became exceedingly popular with the provincials, and at their request impeached Verres for misgovernment in 70 B.C. Verres withdrew into exile without waiting for the verdict of the court. Cicero filled the curule aedileship in 69 B.C., and the praetorship three years later, when he warmly supported the Manilian Law in favour of Pompeius. In politics Cicero occupied a middle position: in his early career he more than once exposed senatorial misgovernment and defended popular leaders, but he never committed himself to the democratic programme; least of all had he any sympathy with the ideas and wishes of the mob. He evinced almost equal dislike to senatorial rule. Belonging to the wealthy middle class, Cicero desired to see the government in the hands of the combined Equites and senate, and it was to this ideal union between the two great orders (*ordinum concordia*) that he devoted himself.

§ **270.** C. Julius Caesar belonged as decidedly to the aristocracy as Cicero did to the middle class; for his family was one of the noblest in the state, and traced back its descent to Aeneas and Venus. He was, however, from the first connected with the democratic party, for his aunt Julia was the wife of Marius, and he himself had wedded the daughter of Cinna. When Sulla assumed the dictatorship he bade Caesar put away the daughter of the dead rebel; but Caesar refused—an attitude which drew from the dictator the remark that "there were many Mariuses in the boy"—and fled to Asia, where at Mitylene he won the civic wreath by saving the life of a fellow-citizen. On the death of Sulla, he returned to Rome, but kept aloof from the premature movement of Lepidus and devoted himself to rhetoric and law-pleading. On the way to Rhodes, whither his studies took him, he was captured by Cilician pirates, but while still at their mercy he threatened that they should pay dearly for the insult, and when he was ransomed by his friends, he returned with a few vessels and crucified the offenders. The next few years were passed in the capital, amid profligacy and excesses of all descriptions: but though this life helped to render Caesar bankrupt, it was powerless to impair his vigour either of mind or body. Shortly before the first consulship of Pompeius and Crassus, he came forward as a leader of the Marian party. He was quaestor in 68 B.C. and praetor in 65 B.C. When quaestor, he exhibited at his aunt's funeral a bust of Marius, and pronounced a glowing eulogy on that great general, although the senate had ordered all portraits of him to be

Caesar, 102— 44 B.C.

§ 271.]   CONDITION OF THE DEMOCRATS.   353

destroyed; and in his aedileship, which he signalized by magnificent games, he angered the government and delighted the populace by setting up on the Capitol those trophies of Marius' Cimbric victories which Sulla had overthrown. As yet, however, Caesar had shown little promise of his coming greatness: he was overwhelmed with debts, and seemed ready to plunge into any scheme, no matter how desperate and dangerous, to secure relief from his poverty. So far was he from his subsequent pre-eminence that at present he was but one among many representatives of an almost discredited party.

§ 271. When the democrats passed the Gabinian and Manilian bills in the teeth of senatorial opposition, they gained a victory which seemed likely to recoil on themselves: for Pompeius, with a triumphant army at his back, was too powerful for a citizen. The popular party endeavoured in his absence to raise up its own chiefs to equal power; and in so doing it could count on the help of Crassus, the representative of the moneyed interest, who had never forgiven Pompeius since the quarrel in their consulship. Should it be necessary to use violence against the government, materials were not wanting. The mob was always ready for a riot; those who had been dispossessed by Sulla longed for an *émeute*; even the Sullan veterans were restless and looked anxiously for fresh campaigns; and there were many young nobles whose politics were determined by their necessities, and who saw salvation only in the abolition of debts (*tabulae novae*) which might result from a successful revolution.

Democratic discontent.

§ 272. The democratic leader most nearly connected with these discontented and reckless groups was L. Sergius Catilina, who returned from governing the province of Africa to seek the consulship at Rome,

Catilina's First Plot.

T. R.   A A

66 B.C. Like Caesar, he was of noble family and sunk in debt, and his career, which he began as one of Sulla's bloodhounds, was in men's estimation stained by the most infamous crimes. An impending accusation for extortion in his province prevented him from standing at the consular elections in 66 B.C., and there were chosen P. Cornelius Sulla, a relative of the dictator, and P. Autronius Paetus. Before the new consuls could enter on their magistracy, they were convicted of bribery—a verdict which carried with it perpetual exclusion from office and the senate. In despair Sulla and Paetus joined Catilina in a plot to overturn the government: L. Aurelius Cotta and L. Manlius Torquatus, the consuls who had taken their places, were to be murdered on their entry upon office; and this blow was to be followed up by making Crassus dictator, with Caesar as his master of horse. Catilina beset the senate-house with a band of ruffians, but the plot miscarried twice.

§ **273**. For some time after this failure at revolution, the popular leaders proceeded by more constitutional means. Caesar tried to get a proposal carried in the comitia that he should reinstate King Ptolemy Auletes of Egypt, who had been ejected by his subjects. Pompeius would thus be kept out of the wealth of the Nile valley, and Caesar would be able to raise a great military force: but this plan also failed. In the summer of 64 B.C., when the consular elections for the following year were in progress, Catilina and C. Antonius Hybrida came forward as the democratic candidates. The senatorial party had no nominees of its own, and was compelled to vote for Cicero, the champion of the Equites and the country folk. In spite of Crassus' money and Caesar's exertions, the new man from Arpinum was returned at the head of the poll. Catilina was not elected

The Democrats and Pompeius.

at all, and Antonius only obtained the second place. Once more the government was safe, for Antonius, a weak and indolent politician, was easily secured by Cicero with the bribe of the province of Macedonia. When the tribunes for 63 B.C. entered on office, the democrats made another effort to secure authority on a great scale. On the plea of providing for poor citizens, the tribune P. Servilius Rullus, proposed the appointment of a Commission of ten men, supported by 200 adjutants of Equestrian rank, with special powers for five years to purchase and allot lands, especially the still undistributed Campanian domain. The funds for buying out the owners of private land were to be found by selling the royal demesnes of conquered kingdoms like Macedonia. No one was to be appointed on the Commission without personally appearing as a candidate. Pompeius was in Asia: therefore his election was an impossibility. Against him would be set Caesar and Crassus, with eight other democratic leaders and 200 moneyed men as supporters, wielding a power over the whole empire as great as was that of Pompeius on the Mediterranean and in the East. Cicero attacked the bill with all his eloquence: the multitude preferred not to take up a position of hostility to Pompeius, and the scheme was frustrated. At the consular elections of 63 B.C. Catilina was again a candidate, but evidently with little chance of success. He knew that Pompeius would soon be back from his conquests, and that if a blow had to be struck, it must be at once. Turning therefore to the discontented throughout Italy—the Sullan veterans, the landless yeomen, the reckless adventurers of the capital, even to slaves and gladiators—he drew together the scattered threads of the conspiracy, and sent C. Manlius, one of Sulla's veterans, to Faesulae to collect a force from the discontented cities of Etruria. But again at the election his programme, despite its democratic and even socialistic features, failed to arouse enthusiasm, and the feeble senatorial candidates won the day.

§ **274**. Catilina appealed to force, but his designs were common property and all the details of the plot had been learnt by Cicero. On October 20 Cicero denounced Catilina in the senate-house, and the consuls were invested with dictatorial power by the customary formula. Before the week was over the insurrection broke out at Faesulae, and on November 1 an unsuccessful attempt was made to surprise Praeneste. On November 8 Cicero convened the senate, and delivered the famous invective known as the First Catilinarian Oration. Catilina felt that he was no longer safe in Rome, and hurried away to Etruria, leaving the conduct of the plot in the city to the praetor P. Lentulus Sura, C. Cethegus, and others of his associates. He was declared a public enemy, and Antonius sent to take the field against him. For some time further the conspirators in Rome made no move: but it was agreed that on the Saturnalia, December 19, there should be a general rising for the purpose of assassinating Cicero and burning the city. But before the plot could take effect, Cicero had secured evidence which incriminated the chief actors in the plot, and was prepared for vigorous measures. The Allobroges in Gaul, who both as a community and as individuals were overwhelmed with debt, sent an embassy to the senate to ask for some relief in their distress. Lentulus, expecting to find ready tools in the envoys, opened negotiations with them and invited them to join in the plot. They professed to assent to his overtures, while revealing everything to the government. They arranged for their own arrest and the seizure of papers compromising the conspirators; and this done, Cicero on

The Second Conspiracy of Catilina.

December 3 arrested Lentulus, Cethegus, Statilius, Gabinius, and others who could not effect their escape. They were put into the custody of leading citizens, for a Roman could not lawfully be either put into bonds or executed. Even Caesar and Crassus were each entrusted with the safeguard of a prisoner. On December 5 the senate met, and debated hotly over their fate: Caesar, while admitting their guilt, did his best to get their lives spared, and seemed at one time likely to succeed, but Cato spoke vigorously for a sentence of death, and his energy decided the question. A few hours later the conspirators were hurried to the Tullianum, and there strangled by order of Cicero. Their condemnation was unconstitutional. It violated the right, which every citizen possessed, of appealing to the people, and Cicero had to suffer for his action at a later date. Early in the month of January, 62 B.C., the troops of Antonius, commanded for the day by M. Petreius, and those of Q. Metellus Celer, closed upon Catilina's small army at Pistoria (*Pistoja*), between Luca and Florentia. The battle was fierce; Catilina fought like a Spartacus, and fell like him amongst 3000 of his men.

Were Caesar and Crassus in the plot? They probably knew of it, possibly they aided it in everything but its worst objects. Crassus, who had more property to lose than any other man in Rome, was not likely to favour a plot which aimed at abolition of debts and general anarchy. Caesar was over head and ears in debt, and might look with more favour even on so extreme an object. An informer implicated both, but perhaps falsely. It was of little moment now. The conspiracy had failed, and Pompeius was more emphatically than ever the greatest power in the state.

§ 275. Whatever the relations of the democrats to the

conspiracy, the defeat of Catilina was a defeat for them too. The Equites, frightened by the attack on property, united, as Cicero wished, heartily with the senate, and even the city mob was disgusted when it learnt that the Catilinarians had proposed to fire their dwellings over their heads. The position of the senate was stronger than it had been for some time past, and the only cloud on the political horizon was the great power of Pompeius. In 63 B.C. Q. Metellus Nepos, an agent of Pompeius, came to Rome to procure for the great general a second consulship and the prosecution of the war with Catilina. The senate, influenced chiefly by the obstinate and unbending Cato, refused both the demands. In spite of this rebuff, Pompeius, though at the head of an overwhelming force, was too honest or too timid to seize his opportunity. He might easily have overturned the ruling oligarchy and, doing what Caesar did thirteen years later, made himself the monarch of Rome. In the autumn of 62 B.C. he landed at Brundisium, but instead of marching on the capital, he disbanded his legions, and after celebrating a triumph in the following year, retired a second time into private life. He had many enemies in the senate, notably Lucullus, whom he had succeeded in the command against Mithradates. He demanded that his arrangements in the East should be ratified as a whole: Lucullus wished each ordinance to be discussed separately. He asked that he might bestow upon his veterans the allotments which they had been promised. In this too he met with a refusal, and the opposition of Cato was so pronounced, that he turned for help to Caesar and the democrats.

The Return of Pompeius.

§ **276.** Caesar was praetor in 62 B.C., and in the following year went out as pro-praetor to Further Spain. When he returned in 60 B.C. he was a wealthy man, and Pompeius was reduced to a nullity in politics. Neither Caesar nor Pompeius was sufficiently powerful to carry out his aims alone; united they might succeed. Accordingly they formed a coalition in the same year, admitting M. Crassus also as a party, because of his useful wealth. Caesar saw clearly that he could never rise to pre-eminence as a mere popular leader with no armed force at his back he resolved now to gain a provincial command, and thereby raise a military power equal to that of Pompeius. It was arranged that Caesar should be consul for 59 B.C., and should while in office gratify Pompeius by carrying those demands which the senate had refused. The senate resisted as far as bribery could help it, and returned a bigoted aristocrat, M. Bibulus, as Caesar's colleague; but, urged on by Cato, it had just quarrelled with the Equites about the contract-price of the Asiatic taxes, and so had lost its most reliable supporters. Caesar immediately introduced three bills—

The First Triumvirate, 60 B.C.

(i) A Commission of twenty was created to allot the Campanian lands among the veterans of Pompeius, and, if necessary, to purchase out of the new Asiatic revenues other lands for distribution.
(ii) The Equites were satisfied by the reduction of their Asiatic tax-contract, which the senate had declined to grant.
(iii) All the proceedings and arrangements of Pompeius in the East were ratified.

The bills were rejected by the senate, and were thereupon submitted to the comitia. Bibulus prorogued the assembly repeatedly on the score of unfavourable omens; but Caesar disregarded both the augurs and the tribunician veto. His adherents came to the poll armed, and carried the bills; whereupon Bibulus shut himself up in his house, and took no part in political business for the rest of the year. Soon afterwards the tribune P. Vatinius brought in a bill (*Lex Vatinia*), which, in imitation of the Gabinian and

Manilian laws, conferred upon Caesar for five years (58—54 B.C.) special proconsular command in Cisalpine Gaul and Illyricum, with three legions. The comitia passed the bill without difficulty, and the senate, as though to salve its injured conceit with a show of carelessness, voluntarily added the province of Narbonese Gaul and a fourth legion. Caesar had obtained what he wanted —a protracted and wide military command; and he cemented his alliance with Pompeius by giving to him his daughter Julia in marriage.

The Vatinian Law, 59 B.C.

§ **277.** Early in 58 B.C. Caesar set out for Gaul, leaving Pompeius to control the unruly elements of the capital—a task for which he was singularly unfitted. The first move of the Triumvirs was to get rid of Cato and Cicero, the most dangerous of their opponents. Egypt and Cyprus had been bequeathed in 86 B.C. to the Roman people, but instead of annexing the former country the senate preferred to recognize Ptolemy Auletes as its king. Cyprus however presented less difficulty, and Cato was sent thither to effect a settlement. The proposer of the bill was P. Clodius Pulcher, a patrician of ruined name and fortune, but of importance to the Triumvirs through his influence with the democrats. For some time he had been the sworn enemy of Cicero. The quarrel arose from the celebration of the rites of the Bona Dea in the house of Caesar, the Pontifex Maximus, 62 B.C. Though the presence of men was forbidden, Clodius, who had an intrigue with Caesar's wife, obtained admittance in the disguise of a female flute-player, only to be detected and expelled. He was tried for profaning the mysteries, but acquitted by a corrupt jury. To revenge himself on Cicero, who had upset his plea of *alibi* at the trial and attacked him in the senate, he got himself adopted into a plebeian family

The Exile of Cicero.

with a view to standing for the tribunate. When tribune (in 58 B.C.) he brought up the never-forgotten execution of Cethegus and his associates. In putting citizens to death without trial, Cicero had violated one of the first principles of the constitution: it was no adequate excuse to say that the sentence was authorized by the majority of the senate. The democrats were eager to revenge the murder of the Catilinarians, and when Clodius introduced a bill " that any one who put a Roman citizen to death without trial should be banished," Cicero, although not mentioned by name, retired from the city into exile. He went to Macedonia, where he spent more than a year in wretchedness, imploring his friends at Rome to obtain his recall.

§ 278. Clodius soon quarrelled with Pompeius by procuring the release of Tigranes, one of that general's Armenian hostage-princes. In the capital, fights, murder, incendiarism, and violence of every kind were of daily occurrence. Clodius headed a regular band of gladiators and ruffians, who terrorized the streets. He found an opponent of congenial temper in T. Annius Milo, who did for the senate what Clodius did on his own or Caesar's behalf. In revenge for the escape of Tigranes, Pompeius supported the oft-debated recall of Cicero. The democrats tried every means to prevent the passing of the bill, but the country voters came up in great numbers, and it was finally carried in 57 B.C. by Milo's aid, after a riot which resembled in its fury the dreadful " day of Octavius " (87 B.C.). Cicero returned amidst the acclamations of all Italy, and the senate welcomed him with open arms. He proved his gratitude by coming forward in the same year to support a bill conferring upon Pompeius the control of the corn-supply for five years. Pompeius did not get the powers he secretly desired, but he fulfilled his commission and relieved the scarcity to which Rome was now continually liable. He made a further attempt to gain military command in 56 B.C., applying for a mandate to interfere in Egyptian affairs ; but the senate was determined that he should not regain the overpowering position from which he had just fallen.

§ **279.** Indeed, the senate was again full of confidence. It saw that the coalition of 60 B.C., besides being intensely unpopular with the democrats, was virtually dissolved, for Pompeius had become jealous of Caesar. Now that Pompeius was no longer an object of fear, it would proceed to humble Caesar. In April, 56 B.C., Cicero proposed that an inquiry should be made into Caesar's Agrarian Law, and L. Domitius Ahenobarbus declared his intention of getting Caesar recalled from Gaul. Caesar, who was well informed of party movements at Rome, retorted by inviting his allies to meet him at Luca in Etruria. Pompeius and Crassus attended, together with more than 200 senators: so large was the party of the Triumvirs. The leaders came to a fresh understanding, and in the course of the following year (55 B.C.) this took effect in the election of Pompeius and Crassus to the consulship, and their immediate action. The tribune Trebonius brought in a measure (*Lex Trebonia*) conferring upon Crassus the command in Syria for five years, on Pompeius the government of the two Spains for the same time. These two provinces were, next to Gaul, the most important in the state. Cato's opposition led to riot and bloodshed, but the bill was carried, and Crassus and Pompeius were once more set up as military powers. Crassus, however, could be relied upon to support Caesar, and was, so far, a counterpoise to Pompeius. In their turn the consuls now proposed a law (*Lex Licinia-Pompeia*) by which Caesar's

The Conference at Luca, 56 B.C.

The Trebonian Law, 55 B.C.

tenure of his province was extended for another five years, that is, until March 1, 49 B.C. This was all that Caesar demanded at present: indeed he seemed to have surrendered voluntarily his own superiority, for Pompeius' new command enabled the latter to raise troops in Italy ostensibly for Spanish service and to keep them there; in other words, to garrison Italia proper, and so endanger Caesar's control of the peninsula. But Caesar was concerned first of all to conquer Gaul, and a few years more would only make his army the more reliable.

Lex Licinia-Pompeia, 55 B.C.

§ **280.** In 54 B.C. Crassus sailed for his province of Syria; Pompeius remained at Rome, sending his legates, L. Afranius and M. Petreius to govern Spain in his absence. But he had no control over the city, despite the troops which he held in readiness, and despite the fact that Clodius was now under the control of Caesar. Riots were of almost daily occurrence, Clodius and Milo were in their element. The consular elections were prorogued by violence for a whole year, and men began to talk of appointing a dictator. At last, in 52 B.C., the two free-lances met in a brawl on the Appian Way. Milo was at the time the senatorial candidate for the consulship, and Clodius was exerting every means in his power to prevent his return for that office. In the fight which ensued Clodius was killed. The populace, enraged at their leader's death, attacked Milo and burned his house, and finally fired the Curia, after depositing Clodius' corpse within it, as a fitting funeral pyre. The senate in despair gave Pompeius his wish—the dictatorship. They called it the "Consulship without Colleague." He immediately called out the Italian levies, made them swear allegiance to his imperium, garrisoned Rome itself, and secured the condemnation and exile of Milo. Again

Murder of Clodius, 52 B.C.

he was monarch in all but name, for Caesar was far away, and moreover was beset by a dangerous rising of the whole of Gaul, and Crassus had fallen at Carrhae in 53 B.C. Pompeius believed he saw his way to getting rid of Caesar for ever; and he first secured the prolongation of his own command in Spain for another five years. Armed with this power he commenced his duel with Caesar.

§ **281.** The Parthians profited by the downfall of the Seleucid monarchy and the humiliation of Armenia, to establish their power firmly as far as the Tigris, on which river stood their capital, Ctesiphon. Between them and the Roman province of Syria there stretched only the plain of Mesopotamia, and it became yearly more evident that hostilities must ultimately ensue. Phraates, the ally of Rome against Tigranes of Armenia, died about 56 B.C., leaving two sons, Orodes and Mithradates, of whom the latter, on being expelled, immediately applied for aid to Aulus Gabinius, now governor of Syria. Gabinius was at the moment occupied in restoring Ptolemy Auletes to the throne of Egypt against the express command of the senate, and when he returned to the Euphrates, Mithradates had been overpowered and put to death, 54 B.C. At this moment Crassus arrived in Syria, and took over the command from Gabinius.

Parthian Campaign of Crassus, 54— 53 B.C.

The richest man in Rome, Crassus at the age of sixty still craved for gold. With him, military command meant opportunity for acquiring further wealth, and the plunder of the East was worth grasping. He spent the year 54 B.C. in pillaging temples and shrines, including that of Jerusalem, and his only military exploit was a reconnaisance into Mesopotamia in which the Parthians were defeated. Encouraged by this success, Crassus, instead of attacking

Parthia by way of Armenia, where his trustworthy ally Artavasdes was king, crossed the Euphrates with seven legions and 4000 horse, and plunged across the desert towards Ctesiphon, 53 B.C. His most trusted adviser was Abgarus, the Bedouin prince of Edessa, who assured him that Orodes was even now in flight with his treasures; and that unless Crassus took the shortest way to his capital, he would lose the spoils he hoped to win. Abgarus was not more sincere than most of his nation. He was playing into Orodes' hands, and led the Romans away from the Euphrates into a trackless, waterless desert. On the plea of dispersing some Parthian horse, he suddenly left them with his cavalry, and the next day the legions found themselves beset on all sides by the entire force of the Parthian lancers and mounted bowmen. P. Crassus, the *Battle of Carrhae, 53 B.C.* son of the Triumvir, perished in an attempt to disperse the enemy, and the survivors of that day were overwhelmed at Sinnaca near Carrhae a few days later, while seeking to reach the Armenian hills. Amongst them fell Crassus himself. The whole Roman force was destroyed; thousands were carried off to live as serfs in Parthia, and not a quarter of the entire number crossed the Euphrates again.

§ 282. There were two causes which made it necessary to take prompt action in 59 B.C. for securing the province of Gallia Narbonensis—the occupation *Caesar in Gaul.* of Eastern Gaul by invading German tribes and the threatened migration of the Helvetii of Switzerland. The most important tribes in Central Gaul were the Arverni, Aedui, and Sequani. The Aedui had shown themselves faithful allies of Rome, and were as a reward placed in a position of superiority over their neighbours. Unable to crush them, the Arverni and Sequani summoned to their aid a restless German horde known as the Suebi, who were anxious to settle in the fertile lands of Gaul. Under their chief Ariovistus, these speedily conquered the Aedui, 71 B.C.; but when they had done so, they began to tyrannize over all the Gauls alike, and to invite other swarms of their kinsmen to cross the Rhine. All the prayers of the Aeduan noble and arch-druid Divitiacus, a friend of Cicero's, failed to obtain aid from the senate. In 61 B.C. the Helvetii of Switzerland, a Celtic people who were harassed by the incessant attacks of the Germans, resolved to quit their homes in a body, and to pass westward to the thinly-peopled but inviting lands between the Garonne and the Pyrenees. The migration was fixed for March 28, 58 B.C., and its course would lie through the Roman province. However indolent the senate might be, and however much averse to giving to any of its great citizens an opening for the acquisition of new laurels in war, action must be taken at once: for if the Helvetii evacuated Switzerland, the Germans would at once take their place and so reach to the very borders of the Narbonese. Accordingly that province was entrusted to Caesar with an additional legion (§ 276).

§ **283.** When Caesar arrived in Gaul, he found the Helvetii on the point of entering the province by the bridge which spanned the Rhone at Geneva. Three of his legions were stationed far away at Aquileia, but he collected what troops he could, gained by a pretence at negotiation a few days wherein to fortify the Roman bank of the river, and repelled the attempts of the Celts to break through by force. They had no choice but to take the longer route, which lay across the Jura Mountains and through the lands of the Sequani. They crossed the Arar (*Saone*) near Chalons, and there Caesar, who had fetched

First Campaign, 58 B.C.

his legions from Cisalpine Gaul, overtook their **rear guard** and cut to pieces one-third **of their host**. A few days later he drew them into battle near **Bibracte** (*Autun*), routed them after a long and desperate struggle, **and** sent the handful of survivors back to their **own land to resume** the work of protecting Switzerland from the **Germans**. This was half his task. Within a few weeks he was hurrying to meet Ariovistus, whom he had peremptorily bidden to recross the Rhine, **and** who had as peremptorily refused to do so. Caesar **was aided** by **the Gallic tribes who** had suffered from the aggressions of the **Germans, but his troops were raw** and timid, **and** he was embarrassed by what threatened **to be** a serious mutiny. Nevertheless, **he utterly** overthrew the Suebi at a spot near Belfort, **and drove Ariovistus and the** few surviving fugitives back into Germania. He spent the winter in Illyricum, which was now **formally reduced to the** shape of a province.

§ **284**. But Caesar had no intention of merely safeguarding Gallia Narbonensis: he was bent on action which should obviate for all time the peril from which he had just saved the province, *Second Campaign, 57 B.C.* and this could only be effected **by setting the** boundary of the empire at **the Rhine**. He left his legions **in winter** quarters among the Aedui as proof of **his** design, and the Gauls understood it as such. When he rejoined **them** in 57 B.C. he learnt that **the** powerful confederacy **of the** Belgae had collected nearly 400,000 men in the north of Gaul in order to drive him back within **the lines of** the province. He instantly assumed **the** aggressive: by playing upon the jealousies of one tribe towards another he won over the Remi (about *Rheims*), the Bellovaci (about *Beauvais*), **and** the Ambiani (about *Amiens*). The more northerly tribes, especially **the** Nervii who dwelt between the Scaldis

(*Scheldt*) and Sabis (*Sambre*), did not submit so easily. They made a desperate assault upon Caesar's army (now raised to eight legions, or 40,000 men, exclusive of Gaulish auxiliaries) when it reached the banks of the Sabis (near *Maubeuge*), and compelled Caesar to fight for his life before he could gain the day. The battle cost them the bulk of their warriors, and they submitted unconditionally.

§ **285.** There remained a third struggle with the tribes of the coast, from the mouth of the Liger (*Loire*) to that of the Rhenus (*Rhine*). Chief among these were the Veneti of Armorica (*Brittany*), an enemy formidable through their skill as seamen and the powerful build of their huge galleys. In the course of a few months Caesar manned a flotilla, the command of which he gave to his legate, D. Brutus. The Romans owed their victory to an expedient whereby they cut the tackling of their enemies, and so disabled and captured their entire fleet. The whole male population was killed or sold into slavery, the excuse being the fact that they had maltreated the Roman officers sent to demand their submission and tribute.

<small>Third Campaign, 56 B.C.</small>

§ **286.** A similar massacre occurred in the following year, when Caesar destroyed the entire mass of two German tribes, the Usipetes and Tencteri, who had ventured to cross the lower Rhine and ask for territories on the Gallic side of the river. Caesar was determined to vindicate the immunity of the Gaulish shore: in ten days he bridged the Rhine near Bonn, and for nearly three weeks ravaged the lands of the Sugambri, as a demonstration of what he could do if he chose. Then returning, he marched across Gaul to the Straits of Dover where a fleet was lying ready, according to orders, to transport his legions to Britain.

<small>Fourth Campaign, 55 B.C.</small>

Britain, originally peopled by non-Celtic tribes, had been occupied by successive waves of Celtic invaders, who kept up communications with their kinsmen in Gaul, and looked with alarm upon the Roman advance. Sailing from Portus Itius (*Wissant*), Caesar made the coast near Romney Marsh, fought his way ashore despite resistance, and advanced for some little way into the country. But there was little spoil to be got and much fighting to be done; his fleet was damaged by a storm, and at the end of a few days he was glad to retire in safety to Gaul. *[First Expedition to Britain.]*

§ 287. The winter was spent in preparations for a second invasion, which was conducted upon a more extensive scale. Landing probably in the same place as before, Caesar fortified a camp on the shore to protect his vessels, and advanced to the river Stour. There he met and routed the Britons, who, in presence of this formidable enemy, had laid aside their customary quarrels, and had appointed Cassivellaunus, king of the Cassi (*Middlesex* and *Hertfordshire*), to be their commander-in-chief. Caesar pushed up the Thames valley in pursuit of his enemy, forced the passage of the river somewhere near Windsor, and took by storm the stronghold of Cassivellaunus at St. Albans. That chief was a good strategist, and his scythe-armed chariots broke the Roman lines; but sedition made easy what would have been otherwise difficult to accomplish: Cassivellaunus, in making himself overlord of Central Britain, had put to death a prince of the Trinobantes (*Essex*), and that tribe forthwith went over to Caesar. Cassivellaunus, deserted by his allies, was glad to make terms, and Caesar, doubtless pleased to end his foray so creditably, returned to Gaul. The Romans boasted that *[Fifth Campaign. Second Expedition to Britain, 54 B.C.]*

they had reduced Britain to the condition of a tributary state, but the tribute was never paid or expected.

The legions were quartered for the winter at various stations throughout Belgica, for the country seemed peaceful, and it was not easy to provision so large a force when concentrated at one spot. But appearances were deceptive. Just before sailing for Britain in 54 B.C., Caesar had been forced to put to death Dumnorix, a noble Aeduan who had been in some degree answerable for the movement among the Helvetii, and had always opposed the Romanizing attitude of his brother Divitiacus. The act had aroused the alarm of the Gauls at large, and taking advantage of the separation of the legions, the Eburones, under their chief Ambiorix, attacked the camp of the legates Sabinus and Cotta at Aduatuca (*Tongres*, near *Liège*), and massacred their troops. They then attempted the like with Q. Cicero, the brother of the orator, whose head-quarters were at Charleroi. But Caesar was too active for them: collecting what forces he could, he suddenly swept upon them from his camp at Samarobriva (*Amiens*), relieved Cicero, and routed his enemies. Labienus, wintering near the Arduenna Silva (*Ardennes*), repulsed the attack of the Treveri and slew their prince Indutiomarus. The lack of united action on the part of the Gauls enabled the Romans to repress the rebellion in detail, but the situation was so serious that Caesar did not as usual spend the winter in Gallia Cisalpina.

Revolt of the Belgae.

In 53 B.C. nothing of importance happened, except a second raid beyond the Rhine into Germany.

Sixth Campaign, 53 B.C.

§ **288.** In 52 B.C. the petty revolts of the preceding years came to a head. All Central and Southern Gaul rose in one last struggle for independence under the headship of

Vercingetorix, one of the royal line of the Arverni. This man had profited by Caesar's successes to learn the Roman methods of warfare: in the power to govern and combine, in rapid movement, and in strategic ability, he was far superior to any enemy whom Caesar had yet encountered. Taking advantage of Caesar's absence in Cisalpine Gaul, where he was holding the usual assizes during the winter months, Vercingetorix made a bold effort to separate him from his army. Only Caesar's greater boldness and the unsurpassed rapidity of his movements enabled him to elude the Gauls and rejoin his ten legions in Central Gaul. Vercingetorix next prepared to meet the legions, but his plan was novel for a Gaul: declining to risk all in one battle, he resolved to lay waste the country and retreat gradually, drawing his enemy after him until want of supplies should give him the victory. But the Gauls could not bear to destroy all their homes: though hundreds of towns were fired and destroyed, they resolved to spare Avaricum (*Bourges*), the capital of the Bituriges and Gaul's chief city, and here Caesar laid siege to a part of their forces. After four weeks the besieged, having in vain tried to break through the Roman lines, were overpowered and massacred. Then Vercingetorix threw himself into his own capital of Gergovia (*Gergoie*), a wellnigh impregnable fortress, and allowed Caesar to attempt another blockade. This time the Romans failed, and the failure was the signal for the Aedui, thus far faithful, to join the revolt. Caesar was forced to form a junction with the army under Labienus, and thus unite his entire force for the overthrow of Vercingetorix, while for the present the rest of Gaul was left to its own devices. Vercingetorix shut himself up in Alesia (*Alise Sainte Reine*, dept. *Côte d'Or*), an isolated hill-fortress of great strength, and no sooner had Caesar

Seventh Campaign, 52 B.C.

drawn round it siege-lines sixteen miles in circumference and of immense strength, than the entire forces of the rest of Gaul enveloped him on the outer side. He was hemmed in between the city and the relieving army, and day after day he had to fight against combined attacks in front and rear. But he held his own, routed the army of relief, and finally forced Vercingetorix to surrender.

§ **289.** Thenceforward Caesar met with little resistance: he ravaged all Belgica and Celtica from end to end, punishing the rebels with the sternest cruelty. When Uxellodunum (near *Cahors*), the last fortress to resist, was at last surrendered, he cut off the right hand of each prisoner (51 B.C.), and so sent them away as an example to others. Success certainly justified his measures; like the Cisalpine Gauls, the peoples of Gallia proper rapidly adopted Roman habits, and when at length the Empire of the West fell, France retained the results of Roman influences to a degree which no other nation could parallel.

<small>Pacification of Gaul.</small>

§ **290.** In 54 B.C. died Julia, the wife of Pompeius and daughter of Caesar, and in the following year Crassus fell at Carrhae. Both these events removed influences that were on the side of peace. While Caesar was engaged in quelling the last struggles of the Gauls, Pompeius and the senate drew closer together and prepared to crush the rival who threatened to destroy both. The position of Caesar was precarious in the extreme: the oligarchs, headed by Cato, had sworn to effect his ruin, and now they were in alliance with the great power of Pompeius. Caesar knew that if he laid down his military authority and entered the city as a private citizen, he might be at once impeached, condemned,

<small>The Question between Caesar and the Senate.</small>

and driven into exile. The command bestowed upon him by the *Lex Licinia Pompeia* expired on March 1, 49 B.C., and as he had been consul in 59 B.C. he could not, in accordance with Sulla's ten-years law, be re-elected for any consulship before that of 48 B.C. The elections would take place in the autumn of 49 B.C.: thus there was an interval of at least six months during which he would be open to attack. He had secured some concessions from Pompeius: he need not personally present himself for election (which would involve the disbanding of his army), and he expected that no successor would be sent to take over his province until January 1, 48 B.C. Both these hopes were overthrown, and on March 1, 50 B.C., the senate began to discuss in earnest the question of superseding him. Caesar made various proposals: he offered to resign everything with the exception of Illyricum and one legion, and again on January 1, 49 B.C., Curio, with his approval, moved in the senate that both Caesar and Pompeius should disband their troops. At this last meeting the consul Marcellus' motion was carried, to the effect that Caesar should give up his army before July 1, 49 B.C. This would leave Caesar a private citizen until the date of the elections. His supporter, the tribune M. Antonius, accordingly interposed his veto. But the extreme party held its ground in the senate, and Pompeius was committed to its support. On January 7 martial law was proclaimed. Caesar's adherents, the tribunes L. Cassius Longinus and M. Antonius, together with Curio, declared that their lives were in danger and fled from the city towards Gaul. Cicero was absent as governor of Cilicia during these events, only returning in time to witness the outbreak of civil war. Since the Conference at Luca, he had submitted to the rule of the Triumvirs: and now all that he desired was peace; but old ties proved too strong, and after much vacillation, he threw in his lot with Pompeius and the senate.

§ **291**. As soon as he heard of the tribunes' flight, Caesar moved across the Rubicon. This river formed the boundary between his province and Italy, and to cross it was equivalent to a declaration of war. People believed that his army was made up of Gaulish savages, but he kept it so well in hand that he won over every one by his moderation. He at once overran Picenum and Umbria. L. Domitius Ahenobarbus occupied Corfinium and endeavoured to stay his progress. Caesar hurried onwards, leaving a small corps to besiege the town, which was soon surrendered by its garrison. All the senators and Domitius himself were at once dismissed free. So rapid were Caesar's movements, so speedy was the change in the attitude of the Italians, that Pompeius lost his head. He had intended to concentrate his troops at Luceria, but he abandoned this design and hurried to Brundisium, in order to cross to Greece. Caesar was unable to overtake him, and the whole Pompeian force with the bulk of the senate crossed to Epirus, and stationed itself at Dyrrhachium. Caesar could not follow, for he had no ships, and besides it was necessary to secure Spain, which threatened his rear. Scarce pausing to seize the state treasures at Rome, he hurried into Spain, where he found himself opposed by L. Afranius and M. Petreius. The armies met at Ilerda (*Lerida*), where Caesar was at first put in great straits for want of supplies; but a few days later he forced the entire force of his enemies to surrender, and thereupon C. Terentius Varro, commanding in Further Spain, did the same. Turning back, Caesar received the submission of Massilia, where Domitius was again defending himself against the

Caesarians C. Trebonius and Decimus Brutus. At the end of the year the conqueror entered Rome, which had been governed for him by M. Aemilius Lepidus, son of the consul of 78 B.C. The people had already declared Caesar dictator, and during the twelve days in which he held the office he passed laws to relieve debtors and the financial distress resulting from the war, as well as a bill to recall the still exiled children of those proscribed by Sulla. On laying down the dictatorship, he was elected consul for 48 B.C.

§ **292.** The war was far from ended: the west was Caesar's, but Africa and all the east was at Pompeius' back. Already it had been necessary to garrison Sardinia to prevent famine in Rome, and with the same object Curio had driven Cato out of Sicily and thence passed to Africa. He was met there by P. Atius Varus, a Pompeian, and Juba, King of Numidia, and killed in battle. In the first days of 48 B.C. Caesar crossed from Brundisium to Epirus, at a season when no one expected that he would attempt the passage. He brought with him 15,000 men, but the rest of his army remained in Italy with M. Antonius for want of ships, and was there kept inactive for some time by the Pompeian fleet under Bibulus. Caesar occupied many Epirot towns, and finding Pompeius entrenched at Dyrrhachium, proceeded to blockade him there. Pompeius, whose forces were much more numerous, broke through the lines, and Caesar, beaten off with the loss of thirty-eight standards, was compelled to fall back on Thessaly for supplies. He had been already joined by Antonius and the remainder of his troops. Q. Metellus Scipio, who was the adopted son of Metellus Pius and father-in-law of Pompeius, was bringing up reinforcements from Asia by way of Macedonia, and Caesar wished to prevent a junction.

Caesar in Greece, 48 B.C.

As he expected, Pompeius followed instead of returning to seize Italy. In this course he was eagerly supported by the mob of senators, who thirsted for vengeance on Caesar, and imagined from the battle of Dyrrhachium that victory was already in their grasp. Near Pharsalus (*Fersala*) in Thessaly, Caesar with 22,000 legionaries routed the army of Pompeius, more than twice as numerous. Fifteen thousand were slain, amongst them Domitius Ahenobarbus, and 24,000 were captured. Pompeius fled to the coast and sailed to Lesbos, where he met his wife and family. Thence he sped to Egypt, where he hoped to find an asylum with Ptolemy Dionysius, son of that Auletes whom Gabinius, the friend and supporter of Pompeius, had set upon the throne. But Ptolemy feared that Pompeius would aid against him his wife and sister Cleopatra, whom he had just expelled from the throne, and he caused him to be assassinated as he was landing.

Battle of Pharsalus, 48 B.C.

§ **293.** Sending M. Antonius back to manage Italy, Caesar hurried with 4000 troops to Egypt, whither he arrived a few days after the murder of his rival. In his need for money he demanded payment of some large debts from the Egyptian crown; but the advisers of Ptolemy were slow to meet the demand, and the Alexandrians, angered by the presence of the legionaries, rose against Caesar and besieged him in the palace. The mob, aided by old soldiers of Pompeius, for a time pressed him so dangerously that he was on the verge of destruction. But at last native reinforcements, consisting of Jews and others, reached him from Syria. The Egyptians were defeated in a battle on the Nile; Ptolemy perished, and his kingdom was given jointly to Cleopatra and a younger brother. But much valuable time had been lost, and it was not until March, 47 B.C., that Caesar could

The Alexandrian War, 47 B.C.

turn his attention elsewhere. Meanwhile Pharnaces, **king of the Bosporus**, a son of the great Mithradates, had taken possession of Armenia Minor and routed Domitius Calvus, the legate whom Caesar sent from Egypt to reduce him to obedience. **Regulating** Judaea and Syria on his way, Caesar hurried to meet him, and at Ziela destroyed his army and took away his crown. It was of this battle that Caesar wrote the famous words, "**Veni, Vidi, Vici.**"

[margin: Battle of Ziela or Zela, 47 B.C.]

§ 294. On the news of Pompeius' death, the Roman populace declared Caesar **again** dictator as well as consul for five years; and they invested him also, as their champion against **Pompeio-senatorial rule**, with the powers and privileges of a tribune for **life apart** from the actual office: a precedent largely used afterwards to establish the principate. Towards the end of 47 B.C. Caesar returned from the East, but soon left the capital for Africa.

[margin: The African War, 47—46 B.C.]

After Pharsalus there was a great scattering among the senatorial chiefs. Cicero returned to Rome, and was pardoned by Caesar on condition that he **retired into** private life. The others—Metellus Scipio, Cato, Gnaeus and Sextus, the two sons of Pompeius, T. Labienus, Caesar's old lieutenant in Gaul—passed to Africa, carrying with them the remnants of the Pompeian army. They united with Varus, the conqueror of Curio, and a force of 120,000 men was rapidly collected. Juba of Numidia, who dreaded the vengeance of Caesar, supported the coalition with his entire cavalry. Late in the year Caesar landed with barely 5000 men. He could not fight with so few: it was necessary to wait for reinforcements. He lay on the coast at Ruspina for that purpose, severely pressed for want of supplies, and harassed by the enemy's cavalry. Towards the beginning of April, 46 B.C., his whole force was collected, and suddenly invested Thapsus (*Demas*). The Pompeian army, commanded by Scipio, gave battle to relieve the town. They left 50,000 dead on the field, in exchange for fifty slain Caesarians. Almost all their leaders fell: Afranius at the hands of the enemy; Metellus Scipio, Petreius, and Cato by suicide. The last-named had fled to Utica, where, on news of Caesar's approach, he read over Plato's *Phaedo* on the soul's immortality, and fell upon his sword. From the place of his death he earned his surname of Uticensis. He was an obstinate and bigoted politician, who clung to old forms when they were effete, and aped the archaisms of his ancestor the censor; but for all that he was the most formidable of the senatorial chiefs, and with his fall the cause of the oligarchy became hopeless.

§ **295**. Caesar returned to Rome and celebrated a magnificent triumph over Gaul, Egypt, Pharnaces, and Juba; for the Roman conscience was not yet so dead as to allow one citizen to triumph over his fellows. After this he received the powers of dictator for ten years and the rights of Comptroller of Morals (*Praefectus morum*) for three years, an office virtually equivalent to the forgotten censorship.

<small>The Spanish War, 45 B.C.</small>

From the slaughter at Thapsus there had escaped T. Labienus and Sextus Pompeius, son of the great Pompeius. They fled to Further Spain, where Gnaeus Pompeius, the elder brother of Sextus, was collecting an army of desperadoes and malcontents; for Spain, never much attached to Caesar, had been estranged by the brutal misgovernment of Q. Cassius Longinus, whom Caesar left as governor of the Further Province after the battle of Ilerda. It became necessary for Caesar to leave Rome again. He landed in Spain late in the autumn, found the Pompeians centralized near Corduba (*Cordova*), and after several months of effort brought them to a pitched battle at Munda. His patience was exhausted: his victory cost the lives of 30,000 of his enemies, including **Labienus**: Gnaeus escaped, to be overtaken and murdered a few days later, while Sextus fled to the mountains and waited for another opportunity (Mar. 17th, 45 B.C.).

§ **296.** The battle of Munda left Caesar undisputed master of the Roman world: open resistance to him was henceforth impossible. He was now free to turn his hand to those reforms in the Government which were indispensable if prosperity was to be restored to the empire. Once Rome had been a community of equal citizens, as remarkable for their simple and temperate life as for their readiness to serve their country honestly in the field and the council-chamber. Now the government of the senate that had led Rome gloriously through the exhausting struggles with Pyrrhus and Hannibal had sunk into an oligarchic system of jobbery and corruption. Now the whole wealth of the empire was in the hands of some two thousand families, while outside this small circle there was nothing to be seen but a starving proletariate and a gigantic population of slaves and freedmen. But if matters were unsatisfactory in the capital, the condition of the provinces was still worse. From end to end of the empire senatorial governors had pillaged and drained the provinces at their will. No justice could be obtained: for if a verdict were given by the law courts in favour of the victims it was rarely enforced, and never in such a way as to recoup the plundered parties. Lands lay idle, roads went to ruin, and trade stagnated. In time of war the evil was still worse: what the governors and tax-gatherers left was destroyed by soldiery billeted at free quarters everywhere. The most

Problems of the Time.

pressing of the problems that Caesar had to solve were therefore these: By what form of government was the oligarchy to be replaced? What measures were to be taken for remedying the social distress prevalent among the citizens? How were the provincials first to be protected against the rapacity of their masters, and secondly to be rendered capable of ultimately sharing in the duties and privileges of citizens?

§ **297**. To Caesar it seemed that the government must be in the hands of one man, and he received a number of offices which made his will supreme in every direction. In 45 B.C. he was made dictator for life; he received the *praefectura morum*, *i.e.* virtually the censorship, for life in the same year; beside this he was granted the consulship for ten years, the tribunician power for life, and the right of voting first in the senate; while by special decrees of the senate he was empowered to decide at his own discretion on war and peace, to dispose of all the armies and treasures of the state, to nominate half the praetors and quaestors, and to appoint governors to the provinces; finally he had been Chief Pontiff, or head of the state religion, since 63 B.C. More important than all, he received in 46 B.C. the title of Imperator for life. As we have seen (§ 49), imperium meant the power of issuing commands to the people in war and in peace, *i.e.* not only did it give to its holder control of the army, but it also made him supreme in all judicial and administrative questions. A consul, however, though the highest magistrate at Rome, held the imperium with limitations: thus he was bound to allow the right of appeal within the walls, and his tenure of authority only lasted for a year. Caesar's imperium was limited neither by time nor by space: for he held it in perpetuity and throughout the empire. The title

Caesar's Government.

of Imperator, in fact, coupled as it was with the tribunician authority and the chief priesthood, gave to Caesar the power enjoyed by the early kings; after a lapse of four centuries, one man was again the general, judge, and priest of the nation. It follows that the senate at once lost the authority it had usurped: in place of controlling the magistrates and so ordering matters at its pleasure, it was now confined to its original functions of giving advice when consulted by the chief magistrate. Its numbers were raised to nine hundred, and among the new members there were many men of low birth, as well as foreigners from Spain and Gaul, so that Caesar apparently intended to convert it into a Great Council which should represent the interests of the whole empire. Some changes were made in the magistracies: the quaestors were increased to forty, the praetors to sixteen, and the aediles to six, and the right of naming (*nominatio*) half of these was reserved to the Imperator. Their independence was lessened in another way when Caesar, by virtue of his imperium, sent out his own legates to command the armies and govern the provinces: the magistrates in fact now became officials of the capital rather than of the empire.

To meet the social distress—the result partly of the civil wars, partly of those economic changes that had been in operation for centuries— *Social Measures.* Caesar carried out some of the reforms which had been advocated by the democrats since the time of the Gracchi. With a view to diminishing the multitude of sturdy beggars who thronged the streets of Rome, he founded across the seas new citizen-colonies, conspicuous among which were the restored Corinth and Carthage; and in a few years he could claim that 80,000 impoverished men had been put in a position to earn an honest livelihood.

An enactment that one-third of the labourers employed on the great cattle-runs in Italy were to be of free birth, tended to preserve the citizen population in the country districts. Others of his measures were by no means so agreeable to the city mob: to their great disappointment Caesar refused to sanction a general wiping out of debts (*tabulae novae*, "fresh account-books"), though he gave debtors some relief; and when he found that no fewer than 320,000 citizens were in receipt of free corn, he lightened the demands on the treasury by reducing that number by one-half.

More important than all else was the question of the provinces. Caesar saw what no Roman had owned, even if he could see it, viz. that if the empire was to endure it must be built up on the vigour and loyalty of the provinces, and that this could only be when the selfish barrier which now separated the citizen from the provincial was removed. As early as 49 B.C. he bestowed the franchise upon the whole of Transpadane Gaul, and one faithful legion, composed chiefly of Gauls, received the same favour in a body. Outside Italy, Gades received a municipal constitution and all the rights of citizenship; and the importance of this concession may be estimated when we remember that such a *municipium* was emancipated from the control of the governor of the province and empowered to manage its own affairs. All Sicily received Latin rights—a preliminary step to the grant of the full franchise. To relieve the poverty of the provincials, taxes were in many cases remitted, and almost everywhere the *publicani* were done away with, by converting the tithes into fixed money payments, and entrusting their collection to the provincials themselves. Finally, the unjust governor had now to consider that he was the servant of a stern

The Provinces.

monarch, not of a corrupt and partial senate, and that for any oppression on his part he was liable to answer at the tribunal of a severe and unrelenting master.

§ 298. Caesar was now bent on asserting Rome's power on the eastern frontier, and on leaving that as secure as he had left the western; for the power of Parthia was yearly growing, and in the glories of new conquests he might at once employ his thousands of restless troops and cause men to forget the civil wars. Slowly but surely the world was settling down to peace and prosperity. Caesar had made all preparations for leaving for the East: he had appointed M. Antonius as prefect of the city during his absence, and to provide against the worst, he had secretly adopted as his son and heir his grand-nephew Gaius Octavius,[1] whose mother was Atia, daughter of Julia, the dictator's sister.

Murder of Caesar, 44 B.C.

There seemed no cause to fear for his safety, while on the contrary there were continually being found fresh means of doing him honour, as when M. Antonius passed a law changing the old name of the month Quinctilis to that of Julius, the name which it has ever since borne. But there were jealous whispers abroad: men said that the show of anger wherewith the dictator had rejected the crown offered to him by that same Antonius was but assumed, and that he would assert himself openly as king. On the Ides of March (Mar. 15th, 44 B.C.) Caesar went down to the senate-house as was his wont. He was beset by a knot of some fifty of his friends and acquaintances, who importuned him to attend to some petition, and refused to be

---

[1] His birth-name was C. Octavius, but upon his adoption he took, as usual, the full triple name of the adopter, and added thereto an *agnomen* showing the *gens* from which he was adopted. In full then his name was C. Julius Caesar Octavianus, and it is as Octavianus that we shall speak of him for the present.

dismissed. A few moments later Rome knew that its dictator was dead, stabbed with a score of wounds by his own familiar friends.

§ **299.** The chiefs of the conspiracy were M. Junius Brutus and C. Cassius: others were Decimus Brutus, C. Trebonius, Casca, Cinna, and Cimber. The mainspring of the plot was Cassius. M. Brutus, a descendant of the famous L. Junius Brutus who had caused the expulsion of the Tarquins, was roused to emulation by the memory of that great deed. Amongst the sixty or so who swore to kill the tyrant, and boasted of themselves afterwards as " Liberators " and " Tyrannicides," there were few but had received high honour and preferment from the man they murdered: Decimus was governor-designate of Cisalpine Gaul and consul-designate for 42 B.C., Trebonius was about to take the governorship of the province of Asia, while Cassius was praetor-designate for 43 B.C. But all were led away by idle dreams of restoring the glorious past of an age when the Romans were fitted to govern themselves—a past long since buried. Caesar's rule was light, but it was the rule of an autocrat, and the fact that his fellow-Romans had themselves voluntarily ratified his usurpation did not make it less a crime in their eyes; while they dreaded the day when he should return from his Parthian campaign, once again a conqueror, and perhaps given over to the pomp and insolence of such sovereigns as those of Parthia and Egypt. They could not see that monarchy alone could save Rome from ruin; they could not see how much Caesar had already done to avert such ruin; they could only hunt after ideals which prevented their recognizing realities. The best proof of their own lack of reason is to be found in the fact that, the deed done, they had made no preparations for future action. Instead of giving back to Rome the energetic

Republic of old, they gave **back** only anarchy, for there was no one to take Caesar's place.

§ **300**. The conspirators had hoped that the **people** would support them. It was a grave miscalculation: Brutus and his companions, finding no one willing openly **to** join them, withdrew to the Capitol; M. Antonius, the consul, persuaded Calpurnia, Caesar's **wife**, to hand over to him all the dead man's moneys and papers; M. Aemilius Lepidus, Master **of the** Horse and **titular** governor of Narbonese Gaul and **Hither** Spain, **marched** into the city with the Caesarian troops which he had at hand, and sided at once with Antonius. At a meeting of the senate (Mar. 17th) in **the** temple of Tellus, Cicero marked his re-entry **to** public life by advising that **an** amnesty should be at once proclaimed: the question as to whether the murderers of Caesar were right or no was conveniently slurred over, while the dictator's acts and legislation were formally declared valid in a body. Had this not been **done**, all who owed to his favours either wealth **or rank**, would have been declared to have no title **to** either—a matter which personally **touched most of the** assassins. As things were, the latter were assured of their safety as far as the senate could guarantee it, and remained in possession of the honours to which Caesar had appointed or designated them. Trebonius **soon** left for his province of Asia, D. Brutus for Cisalpine Gaul; Brutus and Cassius waited to complete their praetorships **before** taking **over** their respective provinces **of** Macedonia and Syria.

Antonius and the Liberators.

§ **301**. The feelings of the people towards their dead hero were clearly shown upon the day of his burial. M. Antonius pronounced over the bier in the Forum the usual panegyric of the **dead**, and read out the terms of the will whereby he declared Octavianus his heir, named many of his murderers as legatees, and left to his fellow-citizens as a lasting souvenir of himself his splendid pleasure-grounds beyond the Tiber, besides a legacy of 300 sesterces per man. The mob was worked up to frenzy, as Antonius desired it should be, and turned to wreak vengeance on the murderers, but most of these had already quitted Rome. In spite of this outbreak, the senate had not lost hope that Antonius and Lepidus might be got out of the way, so that it could resume the reins of government. But Antonius was master of the situation, and had no mind to be so disposed of: he intended to take for himself the place from which Caesar had fallen, and it seemed likely to be easily done by help of the legions and the people. Meantime he professed all loyalty to the senate, as did also Lepidus, and pleased them by moving the abolition of the title of dictator. Next he proceeded to make use of the papers which Calpurnia had put into his hands, by quoting these as authority for any wish or act of his own, under cover of the senatus-consultum of Mar. 17th, whereby all Caesar's deeds were declared valid. In this way he purchased friends in all quarters: to towns and states he granted remissions of taxes; to individuals he sold honours and privileges; and when there was not forthcoming anything in Caesar's handwriting to support some new measure, he hired the services of a forger to make good the want. The senate found that it had only changed one master for a worse. Antonius had as much reason to fear the Liberators as Caesar had, and to prevent their securing the command of large and wealthy provinces he obtained, avowedly on the strength of some notes of Caesar's, the assent of the people to a law whereby his brother, C. Antonius, received for the year 43 B.C. the province of

Antonius Master of Rome.

Macedonia, and Dolabella, his colleague in the consulship, received Syria, the appointments of Brutus and Cassius being cancelled, while he himself replaced D. Brutus as governor of Cisalpine Gaul. The **senate fretted, but it was** forced to look on at the disarming of its instruments.

§ **302.** In April Octavianus, Caesar's heir, now nineteen **years of age, had arrived** in Rome from the camp **at** Apollonia, where he had been in readiness **for** the Parthian Expedition. He found that Antonius had already spent all Caesar's treasure, but by aid of loans he was able to pay the largess of 300 sesterces, and thereby at once gain popularity **with the** people. He would be a powerful **antagonist to** Antonius, if **only he** could be induced to support **the senate in** earnest. Cicero saw this, and abandoning his intention **of** leaving Italy, resolved to throw himself **vigorously into** the struggle. In **the famous** *Philippics* he made a fierce attack on the whole policy of Antonius, and the effect of these speeches **was** so telling that Antonius soon after left for Cisalpine Gaul, hoping to establish himself there as Caesar had done before him and **so to** dominate Rome. But Cicero's animosity encouraged the senate **to** declare illegal his recent redistribution **of provinces, and any** molestation of Decimus an act of treason. The consuls for 43 B.C., Aulus Hirtius and C. Pansa, were ordered **to defend** Decimus. Brutus and Cassius had already left **Italy to take** forcible possession of Macedonia and Syria.

Appearance of Octavianus.

§ **303.** Antonius was desperate. He attacked Decimus and shut him up within Mutina (*Modena*). The consuls supported by Octavianus hurried to the rescue, fought a double battle at Forum Gallorum (Ap. 15th, 43 B.C.) **and** Mutina (Ap. 27th), and raised the siege. Unfortunately both Hirtius and Pansa

Battle of Mutina, 43 B.C.

died of their wounds, leaving the command with Octavianus. While Antonius retreated towards Narbonese Gaul, where Lepidus was still in secret friendly towards him, Octavianus marched on Rome with his legions and compelled the senate to give him the consulship. Soon afterwards he broke altogether with the senate and formed an alliance with Antonius and Lepidus. In November 43 B.C. the three—Octavianus, Lepidus, and Antonius—were declared Commissioners for the regulation of the Commonwealth (*triumviri reipublicae constituendae*)[1] for a period of five years. They represented no party and no interest but their own, to further which they at once proscribed 300 senators and 2000 equites, including M. Cicero and his brother Quintus (Dec. 7th). The great orator was killed near Formiae by Antonius' emissaries; his head was carried to Rome and nailed to the Rostra. The triumvirs next turned to get rid of Brutus and Cassius, to whom fled those of the party of liberty who dared not remain in Italy.

§ 304. Cassius and Brutus had established themselves firmly in their respective provinces while the parties were quarrelling in Italy. Dolabella had been defeated and killed by Cassius; Brutus compelled the surrender of the entire force of C. Antonius, the triumvir's brother. They possessed between them an army of 80,000 foot and 20,000 horse, to provide funds for which they ransacked and plundered the states of Asia without mercy. In the spring of 42 B.C. they concentrated their troops at Philippi near the Thracian frontier of Macedonia, whither Octavianus and M. Antonius had come to meet them, leaving the third Triumvir Lepidus to act as prefect of the city. The army of the Liberators

Battle of Philippi, 42 B.C.

---

[1] Unlike the first Triumvirate, the second Triumvirate was recognized by the people, and the title given by means of a law.

was the stronger, but it lacked supplies, for the **seas were** in the power of the Triumvirs. There were two battles of Philippi: in the former, Cassius was defeated and killed himself, while Brutus' division was victorious; twenty days later the second battle ended **in** Brutus' suicide and the annihilation of his force. The few who did not **choose to** submit to the Triumvirs fled to the west, where **Sextus** Pompeius had emerged from his Spanish hiding-place, **and** with a pirate fleet was scouring the Tyrrhenian Sea **and** threatening Rome with a corn-famine. The **victorious** commanders divided the **world between them**: Antonius undertook to chastise the Parthians, who **were** again ravaging Asia, and there to raise fresh money to satisfy the demands of the legions; Octavianus returned **to** Italy as governor of the west; Lepidus, at all times a mere makeweight, was named ruler of Africa.

§ **305.** The troubles of Italy were **not** yet ended. The ceaseless allotment of lands to successive batches of veterans roused all classes against Octavianus, **who** nevertheless could not otherwise retain that allegiance of the troops which was his sole safeguard. Moreover he was in feeble health, and few expected him to live long; while of his colleagues, Lepidus was incensed at the manner in which he was neglected, **and** Antonius had a brother Lucius (now consul, 41 B.C.) and a wife Fulvia in Rome who desired to see him sole ruler. These two placed themselves at the head of the evicted Italian landowners and the dissatisfied part of the legionaries, and drove the prefect Lepidus out of Rome; but the arrival of Octavianus compelled them to fall back upon Perusia. There, after a siege of many months, L. Antonius capitulated, and so ended the Perusine **War** (40 B.C.); but this collision with his colleague's brother was not calculated to keep Octavianus on amicable terms with M. Antonius in the East. The refugees from Perusia fled some to M. Antonius, some to Sicily to swell the numbers of Sextus Pompeius' followers.

§ **306**. The fortunes of Sextus were prospering rapidly. While in person he cruised in the Lower Sea, and kept Octavianus and Rome in constant uneasiness as to their supplies, his lieutenant Domitius Ahenobarbus was on the Upper Sea equally a source of trouble to Antonius, now in Greece. As the relations between Octavianus and Antonius became daily more strained, Sextus and Domitius found themselves the object of overtures from both, for they had the power with equal facility to keep Antonius out of Italy or to aid him in landing there. Antonius had settled the affairs of the East, but for some months past he had wasted his time and talents upon Cleopatra, to whom he was a complete slave. The fall of his brother Lucius and the appeals of Fulvia at last brought him to see that Octavianus bid fair to oust him, as he had already ousted Lepidus, from any real share in the Triumvirate; and without waiting for any further excuse, he massed his forces in Greece, won over Domitius and Sextus Pompeius to his side, and suddenly descended upon Brundisium (40 B.C.). But just about this time died his wife Fulvia, whose intrigues, prompted by the desire to win back her husband at any cost from Cleopatra, were the chief cause of Antonius' activity. By the efforts of C. Asinius Pollio, Octavianus was enabled to patch up a new treaty with his rival: while Lepidus was allowed to retain Africa, these two divided the rest of the world between them, Scodra (*Scutari*) in Illyricum being the meridian of division. Such was the Treaty of Brundisium (40 B.C.), which was sealed by the marriage of Octavianus' sister

Sextus Pompeius in Sicily.

Octavia to Antonius. To the Triumvir of the East was entrusted the task of chastising the Parthians: Octavianus was to deal with Sextus Pompeius. But Antonius soon drifted back to Alexandria and Cleopatra, leaving his lieutenant Ventidius to conduct operations against the Parthians, who had again overrun all Syria.

§ 307. Meanwhile Sextus, disowned by all parties, seized Corsica and Sardinia, and commenced a blockade of Ostia, whereby Octavianus, who had no serviceable fleet, was compelled to grant temporary terms. By this, the Treaty of Misenum, Sextus received the powers of a proconsul in Sardinia, Corsica, Sicily, and Achaea for five years—that is, he was virtually acknowledged as the equal and ally of the Triumvirs. But within a few months the quarrel was renewed. Antonius refused to surrender Achaea, and when Sextus' vice-admiral Metrodorus put Sardinia and Corsica into the hands of Octavianus, the latter retained them, and Sextus declared war. Octavianus suffered several reverses before he entrusted the war to his lieutenant M. Vipsanius Agrippa, who had recently crushed some risings on the Rhine frontier and in Aquitania (39, 38 B.C.). He took in hand his new duties with energy, and after a year's effort, could put to sea with a force sufficient to confine Sextus to the seas about Sicily. Lepidus landed upon that island with his African legions, while Octavianus attacked it from the north. There was, however, no success until Agrippa in person took the command. He routed one fleet off Mylae, and revenged a subsequent double defeat of Octavius' squadron by a victory at Naulochus (36 B.C.) so crushing that Sextus gave up the struggle and fled to Lesbos. He hoped to find support from Antonius, between whom and Octavianus there had arisen fresh soreness in the preceding year (37 B.C.). Octavia's

Fall of Sextus Pompeius.

influence availed to reconcile the two: by the Treaty of Tarentum the Triumvirs had prolonged for themselves their office for another term of five years, and had united to crush Sextus, Antonius lending a fleet in exchange for two legions to be employed by Ventidius against Parthia. The last act of the naval war came when Lepidus made a fatuous effort to take for himself what Sextus had lost. The attempt was easily crushed, and Lepidus was captured; but Octavianus was content to banish him to Circeii, and to take over Africa for himself (36 B.C.). Antonius made no effort to prevent the fall of the third member of the Triumvirate or to avenge it. He was busy at present on the Euphrates. Sextus, meeting with no aid from Antonius, recommenced his career as a free-lance in Asia, where he was speedily captured and put to death (35 B.C.).

§ **308.** For a few years there was a respite from civil war: on the one hand Antonius was too much occupied with alternate dissipation at Alexandria and campaigning against Parthia; on the other, Octavianus was busy abroad with a rising of the northern tribes—the Salassi and Taurisci of the Pennine Alps, the Liburni of the coast eastward of Istria, the Iapydes and Pannonians—while at home he lost no occasion of rousing the indignation of the Romans against the un-Roman conduct of his colleague. By the year 34 B.C., the north-eastern frontier of Italy was safe; and in the same year Antonius, to revenge a disastrous repulse inflicted two years before by the Parthians, had overrun the whole of Armenia and captured its king Artavasdes; but his conduct in celebrating a mock triumph at Alexandria, acknowledging as his sons the offspring of Cleopatra, and making a will which disposed of whole kingdoms in favour of the children of the foreign woman, had utterly alienated

Relations between Octavianus and Antonius.

the feelings of Rome. Cleopatra urged him to re-assert his rights: she promised him her support in men and money, and bade him strike while there was yet time.

§ 309. In 33 B.C. envoys from Antonius made complaint that Sextus Pompeius had been unfairly driven from the position accorded to him by the Treaty of Misenum (39 B.C.), and that Octavianus was allotting the whole available land of Italy to his own veterans without considering the claims of Antonius' troops. Octavianus replied by complaining that Antonius was answerable for Sextus' death, and that his troops were well provided for by the enormous conquests which their commander claimed to have made beyond the Euphrates. At the close of 32 B.C. Antonius massed in Greece his legions, supported by a fleet of 500 galleys, mostly furnished by Cleopatra, and upwards of 100,000 Asiatic allies. Octavianus had only his own legionaries to aid him, but he had Agrippa for his adviser, and no love-affair to unnerve his judgment. He forestalled Antonius' attack by crossing unexpectedly into Greece, and the two armaments confronted each other for many weeks at the promontory of Actium (*Akri*), on the Gulf of Ambracia. There (Sept. 2, 31 B.C.) occurred the decisive battle. Antonius, finding his Asiatic allies and even his Roman officers constantly growing less trustworthy, while his legions murmured at Cleopatra's presence and her mastery over him, was forced at last to bring his fleet into action. It was twice as numerous as the rival flotilla under Agrippa, but less skilfully manned and handled; yet even so it was only the flight of Cleopatra in the heat of the engagement, and Antonius' senseless imitation of her example, which lost the day. The two made all speed to Egypt, while such part of their fleet as was not destroyed by Octavianus' fire-ships, was surrendered, with the entire land army, to the victors.

§ 310. Leaving Agrippa to return to Rome to control affairs in the capital, Octavianus with a few picked legions proceeded across Greece and through Asia Minor towards Egypt. Cleopatra awaited his arrival in Alexandria: her first impulse had been to fly to the far East, but she had neither allies nor trustworthy troops, and she now resolved to face Octavianus, and attempt to make of him such another conquest as she had made of Antonius. But her artifices were thrown away: her conqueror showed no sign of weakness, and to avoid being paraded in a Roman triumph, Cleopatra killed herself shortly after. Antonius, upon a false report of her death, had likewise made an end of his life, 30 B.C. Thus was Caesar's heir saved the difficulty of dealing with his two last enemies: he could now feel that he was safe. He had saved Rome, and Rome quietly acknowledged the debt. From the day of Actium dates the *de facto* existence of the Principate, and the *de facto* recognition of Octavianus as the first of the Emperors.

Death of Antonius, 30 B.C.

CHAPTER XI.

CONCLUSION.

§ 311. Settlement of Asia.—§§ 312, 313. Titles and Powers of Augustus.—§ 314. Concluding remarks.

§ 311. Octavianus' first care was the regulation of Egypt. It was a country whose occupation by a political rival would be exceptionally dangerous, for its wealth was great, it was strongly situated between sands and seas, and any interruption in its export of corn would reduce Rome to famine. Octavianus therefore refused the senate any share in its government: he placed over it a man of equestrian rank only, and absolutely forbade any senator to set foot on its soil without obtaining his permission. He then journeyed back through Syria and Asia Minor. He made little alteration in the settlement of Pompeius. Few of the native princes had identified themselves with the cause of Antonius: it was therefore both prudent and just to leave them in possession of their sovereignties. Polemo of Pontus, Deiotarus of Paphlagonia, and Amyntas of Galatia were confirmed in their kingdoms, and Herod of Judaea, one of the most formidable of Antonius'

Settlement of Egypt and Asia.

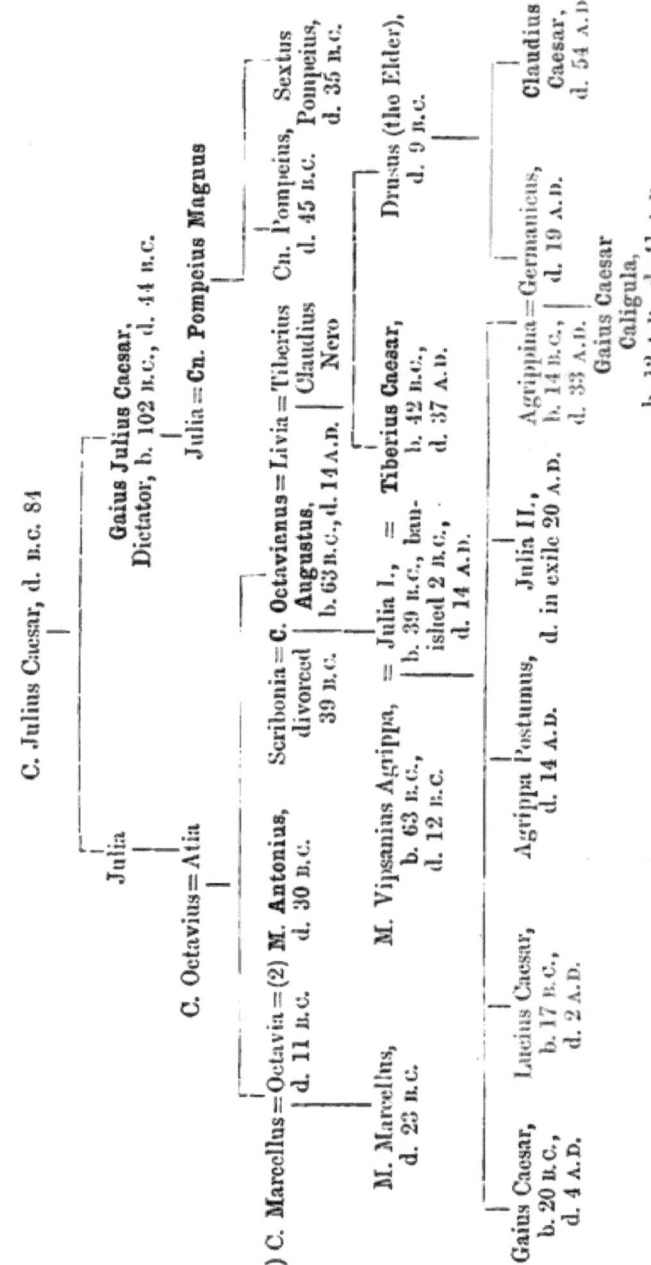

allies, was rewarded by an accession of territory for the instant transfer of his allegiance to Octavianus. Further east, the important kingdom of Armenia was held in check by the Parthian empire, which continually threatened to reduce its weaker neighbours to vassalage.

§ 312. While Octavianus was still in Asia, the senate decreed many honours to the conqueror of Actium. There was accorded to him the privilege of wearing on all public occasions the insignia of triumph— the scarlet robe and laurel wreath; quinquennial games were instituted in his honour at home and in the provinces; his name was inserted in the prayers for the safety of the senate and people; and his birthday was celebrated with sacrifices. When he returned to Rome in the summer of 29 B.C. Octavianus, in emulation of Pompeius and Caesar, enjoyed a threefold triumph. Every one wished for peace, and that desire was gratified by the public ceremony of closing the gates of the Temple of Janus for the third time since its foundation. To reward his legionaries, he presented each with a thousand sesterces—a sum for which the recent spoils of Alexandria gave him enough and to spare. At the same time a largess of four thousand sesterces was given to every citizen, and the public distribution of corn was continued on a more lavish scale than ever. The higher ranks were gratified by appointments to the great magistracies; such senatorial families as had sunk into poverty were rehabilitated by munificent grants; throughout the city the temples and historic monuments were beautified and restored, and public works —such as the famous Temple of Apollo on the Palatine, with its museum and library—were undertaken on the most lavish scale.

§ 313. Octavianus had already laid aside the irregular

title of Triumvir, which indeed no longer possessed any meaning; but he was still consul, and he had been invested with tribunician authority (36 B.C.). In addition, he had assumed the style of Imperator. He wished by apparent deference to the old constitutional formulas to induce the senate to confirm and enlarge the powers he possessed. In this endeavour he encountered no resistance. When at the beginning of 27 B.C. he declared in the senate that his work was done, and that he would lay down the extraordinary dictatorial powers surviving from the triumvirate, the offer was welcomed, but in place thereof the senators decreed him the *proconsulare imperium* for a space of ten years. Octavianus declined to receive it for life, for such an act would have savoured too much of the despotic power of Julius; neither would he accept it over the whole extent of the Roman world, as his great-uncle had done. He handed over to the control of the senate the more peaceful provinces, and retained only such as required the presence of an armed force. According to the theory of the constitution, the censorial powers were inherent in the consul: he was thus enabled when consul for the sixth time in 28 B.C. to revise the list of senators, and in this way to expel unworthy members who had crept into the senate during the troubles of the past twenty years. As he inscribed his own name first on the roll, he became Princeps Senatus, or Head of the House. The title implied no special duties or powers, but was merely a complimentary designation of the most illustrious member in that assembly. It must be distinguished from the title of Princeps, which Octavianus later assumed, and which came to be the Roman equivalent for our word emperor, though it merely described Caesar as *primus inter pares*, the leading citizen in the whole citizen body. From this time dates the regular Principate—the joint government of the emperor and the restored senate. A few weeks later Octavianus received the title of Augustus, by which he has ever since been known.

§ 314. Thus, after a century of revolution, the Roman people finally accepted the government of a monarch. Henceforward there was no serious attempt to restore the old order of things, for the masses readily took part with one who studied to demean himself as a democratic ruler, while the nobles, impoverished and decimated by war and proscription, perforce submitted to a stronger than themselves. When Augustus died forty years later, the undisturbed accession of his chosen heir Tiberius proved how firmly the idea of monarchy was established, and how familiar it had already become to the nation. It was the life's work of Augustus to repair the mischief caused by the troubles of the previous century—to unite, consolidate, and fortify. He waged few wars, and these but upon a small scale, and mostly such as were needful for securing the peace of his provinces and the continuity of his frontiers. Thus, in Spain the Cantabri, Vaccaei, and Astures of the northern mountains for nine years resisted his arms, while the establishment of a "scientific frontier" in the direction of Germania and the north, led to a long and sometimes bloody struggle. But the Princeps achieved his purpose: in every direction he made his influence felt for good, purifying the administration and the law-courts, checking immorality and license, encouraging literature and art and agriculture, reviving decayed industries and developing new lines of commerce; so that even if there were still to be found in Rome a few who mourned for Brutus and Cassius as "the last of the Romans," to Italy and to the provinces

Conclusion.

at large the new Era was one of unqualified relief, security, and progress alike social and political and moral. The means and methods which produced such great results are no part of this narrative: they belong to the history of the reign of C. Julius Caesar Octavianus Augustus, first Princeps, who dated the years of his reign from January 27 B.C.

It must not be forgotten that the monarchy was no new thing. Sulla and Caesar had each for four years been as absolutely monarchs of Rome as was Augustus. The two Gracchi, Marius and Cinna, Pompeius and Antonius, had severally attained for a moment to a similar position. It was only in its stability and continuity, and in the general acquiescence of those subject to it, that the power of Augustus was new. Nor was there any sweeping away of old formulas and instruments of government. Hereafter, as heretofore, there were to be consuls, praetors, tribunes, senate, and all the accustomed machinery of government. The Emperor himself might be consul, censor, or tribune, and so on, in authority if not in name. The revolution was in fact to a great extent the restoration of the old harmonious republican government, long since impaired by the quarrels of parties and party leaders. It was as the "Restorer" of the ancient order of things that Augustus most desired to appear, and so tactfully did he maintain this attitude that none perceived, until the thing was done, how complete and legal was the sovereignty that he built up under the pretence of a general supervision over those officers and offices which he professed to "restore" and protect.

Select List of Books

IN THE

University Tutorial Series

PUBLISHED AT THE

UNIVERSITY CORRESPONDENCE COLLEGE PRESS

(W. B. CLIVE, 13 BOOKSELLERS ROW, STRAND, W.C.)

CONTENTS.

	PAGE
LATIN AND GREEK CLASSICS	3-5
LATIN AND GREEK GRAMMARS, ETC.	6
ROMAN AND GRECIAN HISTORY	7
FRENCH	8
ENGLISH HISTORY	8
ENGLISH LANGUAGE AND LITERATURE	9
ENGLISH CLASSICS	10
MENTAL AND MORAL SCIENCE	11
MATHEMATICS AND MECHANICS	12, 13
SCIENCES	14, 15
DIRECTORIES—THE UNIVERSITY CORRESPONDENT	16

A List of Books for London University Students, classified for the various Examinations, List of Books for the Cambridge and Oxford Locals and the College of Preceptors Examinations, and also the Complete Catalogue of the University Tutorial Series, may be had post free on application to W. B. CLIVE, University Correspondence College Press Warehouse, 13 Booksellers Row, Strand, W.C.

DECEMBER, 1894.

The University Tutorial Series.

General Editor: WILLIAM BRIGGS, M.A., LL.B., F.C.S., F.R.A.S.
Classical Editor: B. J. HAYES, M.A.

The object of the UNIVERSITY TUTORIAL SERIES is to provide candidates for examinations and learners generally with text-books which shall convey in the simplest form sound instruction in accordance with the latest results of scholarship and scientific research. Important points are fully and clearly treated, and care has been taken not to introduce details which are likely to perplex the beginner.

The Publisher will be happy to entertain applications from Schoolmasters for specimen copies of any of the books mentioned in this List.

SOME PRESS OPINIONS.

"The special use of such manuals as those published by the University Correspondence College is that they help the student to systematise his knowledge, and also indicate clearly and definitely the plan to be pursued."—*Journal of Education.*

"This series of educational works, now almost forming a scholastic library in itself."—*Educational Review.*

"The more we see of these excellent manuals the more highly do we think of them."—*Schoolmaster.*

"We have often had occasion to speak in terms of high praise of the University Correspondence College Tutorial Series."—*Board Teacher.*

"As near perfection as can be desired."—*Teachers' Aid.*

"This valuable library."—*School Board Chronicle.*

"This excellent and widely appreciated series."—*Freeman's Journal.*

"The notes have the merit of brevity and practical directness."—*Guardian.*

"As usual with the series, little is omitted that might have found a place in the books, and no point seems unbroached."—*Educational Times.*

"The work of men who have proved themselves to be possessed of the special qualifications necessary."—*School Guardian.*

"By this time every one knows the material and uniform excellence of this series."—*Practical Teacher.*

"The evident care, the clearly conceived plan, the genuine scholarship, and the general excellence of the productions in this series, give them, for the special purpose they are intended to accomplish, high claims to commendation—especially the commendation of diligent use."—*Educational News.*

"This useful series of text-books."—*Nature.*

"Has done excellent work in promoting higher education."—*Morning Post.*

Latin and Greek Classics.

(See also page 4.)

Caesar.—Gallic War, Book I. By A. H. ALLCROFT, M.A. Oxon., and F. G. PLAISTOWE, M.A. Camb. 1s. 6d.

"A clearly printed text, a good introduction, an excellent set of notes, and an historical and geographical index, make up a very good edition at a very small price."—*The Schoolmaster.*

Cicero.—De Amicitia. By A. H. ALLCROFT, M.A. Oxon., and W. F. MASOM, M.A. Lond. 1s. 6d.

Cicero.—De Senectute. By the same Editors. 1s. 6d.

"The notes, although full, are simple."—*Educational Times.*

Horace.—Odes, **Books I.—III.** By A. H. ALLCROFT, M.A. Oxon., and B. J. HAYES, M.A. Lond. and Camb. 1s. 6d. each.

"Notes which leave no difficulty unexplained."—*The Schoolmaster.*

"The Notes (on Book III.) are full and good, and nothing more can well be demanded of them."—*Journal of Education.*

Livy.—Book I. By A. H. ALLCROFT, M.A. Oxon., and W. F. MASOM, M.A. Lond. *Third Edition.* 2s. 6d.

"The notes are concise, dwelling much on grammatical points and dealing with questions of history and archæology in a simple but interesting fashion."—*Education.*

Vergil.—Aeneid, Book I. By A. H. ALLCROFT, M.A. Oxon., and W. F. MASOM, M.A. Lond. 1s. 6d.

Xenophon.—Anabasis, Book I. By A. H. ALLCROFT, M.A. Oxon., and F. L. D. RICHARDSON, B.A. Lond. 1s. 6d.

"The notes are all that could be desired."—*Schoolmaster.*

The above editions of LATIN and GREEK CLASSICS are on the following plan:—

A short INTRODUCTION gives an account of the Author and his chief works, the circumstances under which he wrote, and his style, dialect, and metre, where these call for notice.

The TEXT is based on the latest and best editions, and is clearly printed in large type.

The distinctive feature of the NOTES is the omission of parallel passages and controversial discussions of difficulties, and stress is laid on all the important points of grammar and subject-matter. Information as to persons and places mentioned is grouped together in an HISTORICAL AND GEOGRAPHICAL INDEX, by this means the expense of procuring a Classical Dictionary is rendered unnecessary.

The **works** in the *Matriculation* series have been edited with a view to meeting the wants of beginners, while the *Graduation* series furnishes suitably annotated editions for the more advanced student. A complete list is given overleaf.

Editions of Latin and Greek Classics.

The following editions are now ready, with the exception of those marked * (in the press), and those marked † (in preparation).

MATRICULATION SERIES.

	s. d.		s. d.
CAESAR—Gallic War, Bk. 1	1 6	LIVY—Bk. 21	2 6
CAESAR—Gallic War, Bk. 5	1 6	*OVID—Heroides 1, 2, 3, 5,	
CAESAR—Gallic War, Bk. 6	1 6	7, 12	2 6
CAESAR—Gallic War, Bk. 7	2 6	OVID—Metamorphoses, Bk. 11	1 6
CAESAR—Gallic War, Bk. 7, Ch. 1-68	1 6	OVID—Tristia, Bk. 1	1 6
		OVID—Tristia, Bk. 3	1 6
CICERO—De Amicitia	1 6	SALLUST—Catiline	2 6
CICERO—De Senectute	1 6	SOPHOCLES—Antigone	2 6
*CICERO—In Catilinam, Bk. 3	1 6	VERGIL—Aeneid, Bk. 1	1 6
CICERO—Pro Archia	1 6	VERGIL—Aeneid, Bk. 3	1 6
CICERO—Pro Balbo	1 6	VERGIL—Aeneid, Bk. 5	1 6
†EURIPIDES—Andromache	3 6	VERGIL—Aeneid, Bk. 6	1 6
HOMER—Iliad, Bk. 6	1 6	VERGIL—Aeneid, Bk. 7	1 6
HOMER—Odyssey, Bk. 17	1 6	VERGIL—Aeneid, Bk. 9	1 6
HORACE—Odes, Bk. 1	1 6	VERGIL—Aeneid, Bk. 10	1 6
HORACE—Odes, Bk. 2	1 6	XENOPHON—Anabasis, Bk. 1	1 6
HORACE—Odes, Bk. 3	1 6	XENOPHON—Hellenica, 3	3 6
HORACE—Odes, Bk. 4	1 6	XENOPHON—Hellenica, 4	3 6
LIVY—Bk. 1	2 6		

GRADUATION SERIES.

	s. d.		s. d.
AESCHYLUS — Prometheus Vinctus	2 6	JUVENAL—Satires, 1, 3, 4	3 6
		JUVENAL—Satires, 8, 10, 13	2 6
ARISTOPHANES—Plutus	2 6	LIVY—Bk. 3	3 6
CICERO—Ad Atticum, Bk. 4	3 6	LIVY—Bk. 5	2 6
CICERO—De Finibus, Bk. 1	2 6	OVID—Fasti, Bks. 3, 4	2 6
†CICERO—De Finibus, Bk. 2	3 6	PLATO—Phaedo	3 6
†CICERO—Pro Milone	3 6	†SOPHOCLES—Ajax	3 6
CICERO—Pro Plancio	2 6	SOPHOCLES—Electra	3 6
HERODOTUS—Bk. 6	2 6	TACITUS—Annals, Bk. 1	2 6
HERODOTUS—Bk. 8	3 6	TACITUS—Annals, Bk. 2	2 6
HOMER—Odyssey, Bks. 9, 10	2 6	TACITUS—Histories, Bk. 1	3 6
HOMER—Odyssey, Bks. 11, 12	2 6	THUCYDIDES—Bk. 7	3 6
HOMER—Odyssey, Bks. 13, 14	2 6	†VERGIL — Georgics, Bks. 1, 2	3 6
HORACE—Epistles	3 6		
†HORACE—Epodes	1 6	*XENOPHON—Oeconomicus	4 6
HORACE—Satires	4 6		

Vocabularies and Test Papers.

The VOCABULARY contains, arranged in the order of the Text, words with which the learner is likely to be unacquainted. The principal parts of verbs are given, and (when there is any difficulty about it) the parsing of the word as it occurs in the Text. The Vocabulary is interleaved with writing paper.

Two series of TEST PAPERS are, as a rule, provided, of which the first and easier series is devoted entirely to translation, accidence, and very elementary points of Syntax; the second, which is intended for use the last time the book is read through, deals with more advanced points.

	s. d.		s. d.
ACTS OF THE APOSTLES ..	1 0	LIVY—Bk. 5...............	1 0
AESCHYLUS — Prometheus		LIVY—Bk. 21	1 0
Vinctus	1 0	OVID—Fasti, Bks. 3 and 4..	1 0
CAESAR—Gallic War, Bk. 1	1 0	*OVID—Heroides, 1, 2, 3, 5,	
CAESAR—Gallic War, Bk. 5	1 0	7, 12	1 6
CAESAR—Gallic War, Bk. 6	1 0	OVID—Metamorphoses, Bk.	
CAESAR—Gallic War, Bk. 7	1 6	11	1 0
CICERO—De Amicitia	1 0	OVID—Tristia, Bk. 1	1 0
CICERO—De Senectute	1 0	OVID—Tristia, Bk. 3	1 0
†CICERO—In Catilinam, Bk. 3	1 0	SALLUST—Catiline	1 0
CICERO—Pro Archia	1 0	SOPHOCLES—Antigone	1 0
CICERO—Pro Balbo	1 0	SOPHOCLES—Electra	1 0
CICERO—Pro Cluentio......	1 0	TACITUS—Annals, Bk. 1....	1 0
†CICERO—Pro Milone......	1 0	TACITUS—Histories, Bk. 1..	1 0
CICERO—Pro Plancio	1 0	VERGIL—Aeneid, Bk. 1....	1 0
EURIPIDES—Ion	1 0	VERGIL—Aeneid, Bk. 3....	1 0
HERODOTUS—Bk. 6........	1 0	VERGIL—Aeneid, Bk. 5....	1 0
HERODOTUS—Bk. 8........	1 0	VERGIL—Aeneid, Bk. 6....	1 0
HOMER—Iliad, Bk. 6	1 0	VERGIL—Aeneid, Bk. 7....	1 0
HOMER—Odyssey, Bk. 17 ..	1 0	VERGIL—Aeneid, Bks. 9, 10	1 0
HORACE—Epistles	1 0	VERGIL—Georgics, Bks. 1, 2	1 0
HORACE—Odes, Bks. 1-4, each	1 0	XENOPHON—Anabasis, Bk. 1	1 0
HORACE—Satires	1 0	XENOPHON — Cyropaedeia,	
LIVY—Bk. 1...............	1 0	Bks. 1 and 5, each	1 0
LIVY—Bk. 3...............	1 0	†XENOPHON, Oeconomicus..	1 0

Latin and Greek.

Grammars and Readers.

Greek Reader, The Tutorial, or PROOEMIA GRAECA. By A. WAUGH YOUNG, M.A. Lond., Gold Medallist in Classics. 2s. 6d.

Higher Greek Reader: A Course of 132 Extracts from the best writers, in Three Parts, with an Appendix containing the Greek Unseens set at B.A. Lond. 1877—1893. 3s. 6d.

The Tutorial Latin Grammar. By B. J. HAYES, M.A. Lond. and Camb., and W. F. MASOM, M.A. Lond. *Second Edition.* 3s. 6d.

"Practical experience in teaching and thorough familiarity with details are plainly recognisable in this new Latin Grammar. Great pains have been taken to bring distinctly before the mind all those main points which are of fundamental importance and require firm fixture in the memory, and the illustrative examples have been gathered with much care from the classics most usually read for examinations. Though full, it is not overcrowded with minutiæ."—*Educational News.*

"It is accurate and full without being overloaded with detail, and varieties of type are used with such effect as to minimise the work of the learner. Tested in respect of any of the crucial points, it comes well out of the ordeal."—*Schoolmaster.*

The Preceptors' Latin Course. [*In preparation.*

Latin Composition and Syntax. With copious EXERCISES. By A. H. ALLCROFT, M.A. Oxon., and J. H. HAYDON, M.A. Camb. and Lond. *Third Edition.* 2s. 6d.

The more advanced portions of the book-work are denoted by an asterisk, and the relative importance of rules and exceptions is shown by variety of type. Each Exercise is divided into three sections of progressive difficulty.

"This useful little book."—*Journal of Education.*

"This is one of the best manuals on the above subject that we have met with for some time. Simplicity of statement and arrangement: apt examples illustrating each rule; exceptions to these adroitly stated just at the proper place and time, are among some of the striking characteristics of this excellent book. Every advantage too has been taken of printing and type, to bring the leading statements prominently before the eye and mind of the reader. It will not only serve as an admirable class-book, but from its table of contents and its copious index will prove to the private student an excellent reference book as well."—*The Schoolmaster.*

"The clearness and concise accuracy of this book throughout are truly remarkable."—*Education.*

"The arrangement and order are exceedingly good."—*School Board Chronicle.*

The Tutorial Latin Reader. 1s. 6d. With VOCABULARY. 2s. 6d.

"A soundly practical work."—*The Guardian.*

Roman and Grecian History.

The Tutorial History of Rome. (To A.D. 14.) By A. H. ALLCROFT, M.A. Oxon., and W. F. MASOM, M.A. LOND. With Maps. 3s. 6d.

"It is well and clearly written."—*Saturday Review.*

A History of Rome from B.C. 31 to A.D. 96: The Early Principate. By A. H. ALLCROFT, M.A. Oxon., and J. H. HAYDON, M.A. Camb. and Lond. 2s. 6d.

"Accurate, and in accordance with the authorities."—*Journal of Education.*

"It is deserving of the highest praise. All that the student can require for his examination is supplied in scholarly shape, and in so clear a manner that the task of the learner is made comparatively easy."—*Literary World.*

A Longer History of Rome. The following volumes are ready or in preparation:—

1. History of Rome, B.C. 287-202: The Struggle for Empire. By W. F. MASOM, M.A. Lond. **4s.** 6d.
2. History of Rome, B.C. 202-133: Rome under the Oligarchs. By A. H. ALLCROFT, M.A. Oxon., and W. F. MASOM, M.A. Lond. 4s. 6d.
3. History of Rome, **B.C. 133-78.** By W. F. MASOM, M.A. Lond. [*In preparation.*
4. History of Rome, B.C. 78-31: The Making of the Monarchy. By A. H. ALLCROFT, M.A. Oxon. 4s. 6d.
5. History of Rome, B.C. 31 to **A.D. 96.** (*See above.*)

A History of Greece. To be completed in Six Volumes:—

1. Early Grecian History. A Sketch of the Historic Period, and its Literature, to 495 B.C. By A. H. ALLCROFT, M.A. Oxon., and W. F. MASOM, M.A. Lond. 3s. 6d.

"For those who require a knowledge of the period no better book could be recommended."—*Educational Times.*

2. *Vol. II. will cover the period* 495-431 B.C.
3, 4. History of Greece, B.C. 431-371. By A. H. ALLCROFT, M.A. Oxon. 6s. 6d. [*In preparation.*
5. History of Greece, B.C. **371-323:** The Decline of Hellas. By A. H. ALLCROFT, M.A. Oxon. 4s. 6d.
6. History of Sicily, B.C. 490-289, from the Tyranny of Gelon to the Death of Agathocles, with a History of Literature. By A. H. ALLCROFT, M.A. Oxon., and W. F. MASOM, M.A. Lond. 3s. 6d.

"We can bear high testimony to its merits."—*Schoolmaster.*

French.

The Tutorial French Accidence. By ERNEST WEEKLEY, M.A. Lond. 3s. 6d.

"The essentials of the accidence of the French Language are skilfully exhibited in carefully condensed synoptic sections."—*Educational News.*
"A most practical and able compilation."—*Public Opinion.*
"The manual is an excellent one—clear, well-arranged, and if not quite exhaustive, at least very fairly complete."—*Glasgow Herald.*
"A simply expounded and serviceable handbook."—*Scotsman.*

The Tutorial French Syntax. 3s. 6d. [*In preparation.*

The Preceptors' French Course. [*In preparation.*

The Preceptors' French Reader. With Vocabulary 1s. 6d. [*In preparation.*

French Prose Reader. Edited by S. BARLET, B. ès Sc., Examiner in French to the College of Preceptors, and W. F. MASOM. M.A. Lond. With VOCABULARY. *Second Edition.* 2s. 6d.

"The book is very well adapted to the purpose for which it is intended."—*Schoolmaster.*
"Admirably chosen extracts. They are so selected as to be thoroughly interesting and at the same time thoroughly illustrative of all that is best in French literature."—*School Board Chronicle.*

Advanced French Reader: Containing passages in prose and verse representative of all the modern Authors. Edited by S. BARLET, B. ès Sc., Examiner in French to the College of Preceptors, and W. F. MASOM, M.A. Lond. 3s. 6d.

"Chosen from a large range of good modern authors, the book provides excellent practice in 'Unseens.'"—*The Schoolmaster.*

English History.

The Tutorial History of England. By C. S. FEARENSIDE, M.A. Oxon. [*In preparation.*

The Intermediate Text-Book of English History: a Longer History of England. By C. S. FEARENSIDE, M.A. Oxon., and A. JOHNSON EVANS, M.A. Camb. With Maps and Plans.

VOLUME I., to 1485. [*In preparation.*
VOLUME II., 1485 to 1603. 5s. 6d.
VOLUME III., 1603 to 1714. [*In the press.*
VOLUME IV., 1685 to 1801. 4s. 6d.

"The results of extensive reading seem to have been photographed upon a small plate, so that nothing of the effect of the larger scene is lost."—*Teachers' Monthly.*
"His genealogical tables and his plans of the great battles are very well done, as also are the brief biographical sketches which come in an appendix at the end."—*Literary Opinion.*
"It is lively; it is exact; the style is vigorous and has plenty of swing; the facts are numerous, but well balanced and admirably arranged."—*Education.*

English Language and Literature.

The English Language: Its History and Structure. By W. H. Low, M.A. Lond. *Second Edition.* 3s. 6d.

CONTENTS:—The Relation of English to other Languages—Survey of the Chief Changes that have taken place in the Language—Sources of our Vocabulary—The Alphabet and the Sounds of English—Grimm's Law—Gradation and Mutation—Transposition, Assimilation, Addition and Disappearance of Sounds in English—Introductory Remarks on Grammar—The Parts of Speech, etc.—Syntax—Parsing and Analysis—Metre—Examination Questions.

"A clear workmanlike history of the **English language done on sound principles.**"—*Saturday Review.*

"The author deals very fully with the source and growth of the language. The parts of speech are dealt with historically as well as grammatically. The work is scholarly and accurate."—*Schoolmaster.*

"The history of the language and etymology are both well and fully treated."—*Teachers' Monthly.*

"Aptly and cleverly written."—*Teachers' Aid.*

"The arrangement of the book is devised in the manner most suited to **the** student's convenience, and most calculated to impress his memory."—*Lyceum.*

"It is in the best sense a scientific treatise. There is not a superfluous sentence."—*Educational News.*

The Intermediate Text-Book of English Literature. By W. H. Low, M.A. Lond.

VOLUME I., to 1558. 3s. 6d. *[In preparation.*

VOLUME II., 1558 to 1660. 3s. 6d.

VOLUME III., 1660 to 1798. 3s. 6d.

Vols. II. and III., bound together, 5s. 6d.

"Really judicious in the selection of the details given."—*Saturday Review.*

"Designed on a thoroughly sound principle. Facts, dates, and representative quotations are plentiful. The critical extracts are judiciously chosen, and Mr. Low's own writing is clear, effective for its purpose, and evidently the result of thorough knowledge and a very considerable ability to choose between good and bad."—*National Observer.*

"It affords another example of the author's comprehensive grasp of his subject, combined with a true teacher's power of using such judicious condensation that the more salient points are brought clearly into view."—*Teachers' Monthly.*

"Mr. Low has succeeded in giving a **very** readable and lucid account **of the** literature of the time."—*Literary World.*

"Mr. Low's book forms a serviceable student's digest of an important period in our literature."—*Schoolmaster.*

"The style is terse and pointed. The representative quotations **are** aptly and judiciously chosen. The criticisms are well grounded, clearly expressed and modestly presented."—*Morning Post.*

A Middle English Reader. By S. J. EVANS, M.A. Lond.
[In preparation.

English Classics.

Addison.—Essays on Milton, Notes on. By W. H. Low, M.A. 2s.

Aelfric's Homilies, Glossary to, in order of the Text. By A. J. Wyatt, M.A. Lond., and H. H. Johnson, B.A. Lond. 2s. 6d.

Chaucer.—Prologue, Knight's Tale. Edited by A. J. Wyatt, M.A. Lond. 2s. 6d. [*In the press.*

Dryden.—Essay on Dramatic Poesy. Edited by W. H. Low, M.A. Lond. TEXT and NOTES. 3s. 6d. Or separately, 2s. each.

Goldsmith.—Poems. Edited by Austin Dobson. 2s. 6d.

Havelok the Dane. A Close TRANSLATION, preceded by the Additional Notes and Corrections issued in Prof. Skeat's New Edition. By A. J. Wyatt, M.A. Lond. 3s.

Milton.—Samson Agonistes. Edited by A. J. Wyatt, M.A. Lond. 2s. 6d.

"A capital Introduction. The notes are excellent."—*Educational Times.*

Milton.—Sonnets. Edited by W. F. Masom, M.A. Lond. *Second Edition.* 1s. 6d.

Saxon Chronicle, The, from 800-1001 A.D. A TRANSLATION. By W. H. Low, M.A. Lond. 3s.

Shakespeare.—Henry VIII. With INTRODUCTION and NOTES by W. H. Low, M.A. Lond. *Second Edition.* 2s.

Shakespeare.—Richard II. Edited by Prof. W. J. Rolfe. (Harper Bros., New York.) 2s.

Shakespeare.—Twelfth Night. Edited by Prof. W. J. Rolfe. (Harper Bros., New York.) 2s.

Sheridan.—The Rivals. Edited by W. H. Low, M.A. Lond. 1s.

"A fully annotated edition . . . complete and thoroughly workmanlike."—*Education.*

Spenser's Shepherd's Calender, Notes on, with an INTRODUCTION. By A. J. Wyatt, M.A. Lond. 2s.

Mental and Moral Science.

Ethics, Manual of. By J. S. MACKENZIE, M.A., Fellow of Trinity College, Cambridge, Examiner in the University of Aberdeen. *Second Edition.* 6s. 6d.

"In writing this book Mr. Mackenzie has produced an earnest and **striking contribution** to the ethical literature of the time."—*Mind.*

"This excellent manual."—*International Journal of Ethics.*

"Mr. Mackenzie may be congratulated on having presented a thoroughly good and helpful guide to this attractive, yet elusive and difficult, subject."—*Schoolmaster.*

"It is a most admirable student's manual."—*Teachers' Monthly.*

"Mr. Mackenzie's book is as nearly perfect as it could be. It covers the whole field, and for perspicuity and thoroughness leaves nothing to be desired. The pupil who masters it will find himself equipped with a sound grasp of the subject such as no one book with which we are acquainted has hitherto been equal to supplying. Not the least recommendation is the really interesting style of the work."—*Literary World.*

"Written with lucidity and an obvious mastery of the whole bearing of the subject."—*Standard.*

"No one can doubt either the author's talent or his information. The ground of ethical science is covered by his treatment completely, sensibly, and in many respects brilliantly."—*Manchester Guardian.*

"For a practical aid to the student it is very admirably adapted. It is able, clear, and acute. The arrangement of the book is excellent."—*Newcastle Daily Chronicle.*

Logic, A Manual of. By J. WELTON, M.A. Lond. 2 vols. Vol. I., 10s. 6d. [*Vol. II. in preparation.*

This book embraces the entire London B.A. and B.Sc. Syllabus, and renders unnecessary the purchase of the numerous books hitherto used. The relative importance of the sections is denoted by variety of type, and a minimum course of reading is thus indicated.

Vol. I. contains the whole of Deductive Logic, except Fallacies, which will be treated, with Inductive Fallacies, in Vol. II.

"A clear and compendious summary of the views of various thinkers on important and doubtful points."—*Journal of Education.*

"A very good book . . not likely to be superseded for a long time to come."—*Educational Review.*

"Unusually complete and reliable. The arrangement of divisions and subdivisions is excellent, and cannot but greatly facilitate the study of the subject by the diligent student."—*Schoolmaster.*

"The manual may be safely recommended."—*Educational Times.*

"Undoubtedly excellent."—*Board Teacher.*

Mathematics and Mechanics.

Algebra, The Intermediate Text-Book of. [*Shortly.*

Astronomy, Elementary Mathematical. By C. W. C. BARLOW, M.A. Lond. and Camb., B.Sc. Lond., and G. H. BRYAN, M.A. Camb., Fellow of St. Peter's College. *Second Edition*, with ANSWERS. 8s. 6d.

"Probably within the limits of the volume no better description of the methods by which the marvellous structure of scientific astronomy has been built up could have been given."—*Athenæum.*

"Sure to find favour with students of astronomy."—*Nature.*

"This book supplies a distinct want. The diagrams are clear, the style of writing lucid, and the mathematical knowledge required but small."—*Teachers' Monthly.*

"Completely successful."—*Literary World.*

"One noticeable feature of the book is that the more important theorems are carefully illustrated by worked out numerical examples, and are so well arranged and clearly written that the volume ought to serve as a good text-book."—*Bombay Advertiser.*

"A careful examination has led to the verdict that the book is the best of its kind. It is accurate and well arranged, and in every respect meets the requirements for which it has been designed."—*Practical Teacher.*

"It is an admirable text-book."—*School Guardian.*

"It will carry a student a long way in the sound study of astronomy."—*National Observer.*

Coordinate Geometry: The Right Line and Circle. By WILLIAM BRIGGS, M.A., LL.B., F.R.A.S., and G. H. BRYAN, M.A. *Second Edition*. 3s. 6d.

"It is thoroughly sound throughout, and indeed deals with some difficult points with a clearness and accuracy that has not, we believe, been surpassed."—*Education.*

"An admirable attempt on the part of its authors to realize the position of the average learner, and to provide for the wants of the private student. . . . Frequent exercises and examination papers have been interspersed, and different sizes of type and intelligently drawn figures will afford great assistance in revision."—*Educational Times.*

"Thoroughly practical and helpful."—*Schoolmaster.*

"Thoroughly sound and deals clearly and accurately with difficult points."—*The Indian Engineer.*

"Another of the excellent books published by the University Correspondence College Press. The arrangement of matter and the copious explanations it would be hard to surpass. It is the best book we have seen on the subject."—*Board Teacher.*

"The authors have had exceptional opportunities of appreciating the difficulties of beginners, and they have succeeded in producing a work which will be found especially useful."—*English Mechanic.*

Mathematics and Mechanics—*continued*.

Coordinate Geometry, Worked Examples in: A Graduated Course on the Right Line and Circle. 2s. 6d.

References are made to the book-work of *Coordinate Geometry*.

Dynamics, Text-Book of. By WILLIAM BRIGGS, M.A., LL.B., F.R.A.S., and G. H. BRYAN, M.A. 2s.

Geometry of Similar Figures and the Plane. (Euclid VI. and **XI.**) With numerous Deductions worked and unworked. 3s. **6d.** [*Shortly.*

Hydrostatics, An Elementary Text-Book of. By WILLIAM BRIGGS, M.A., LL.B., F.R.A.S., and G. H. BRYAN, M.A. [*Shortly.*

Mechanics and Hydrostatics, Worked Examples in: A Graduated Course on the London Matriculation Syllabus. 1s. 6d.

"Will prove itself a valuable aid. Not only are the worked **examples well graded,** but in many cases explanatory paragraphs give useful hints **as to processes. The** book has our warm approbation."—*Schoolmaster.*

Mensuration and Spherical Geometry: Being Mensuration of the Simpler Figures and the Geometrical Properties of the Sphere. By WILLIAM BRIGGS, M.A., LL.B., F.R.A.S., and T. W. EDMONDSON, B.A. Lond. and Camb. 3s. 6d.

"Although intended to meet the requirements of candidates for particular examinations, this book may be used generally with safety. The chief feature in it appears to be the inclusion of proofs of all formulæ presented. It is thus far more than a mere collection of rules and examples."—*Educational Times.*

"The book comes from the hands of experts; we can think of nothing better qualified to enable the student to master this branch of the syllabus, and what is more important still, to promote a correct style in his mathematical manipulations."—*Schoolmaster.*

Mensuration of the Simpler Figures. By WILLIAM BRIGGS, M.A., F.R.A.S., and T. W. EDMONDSON, B.A. Lond. and Camb. 2s. 6d.

Statics, Text-Book of. By WILLIAM BRIGGS, M.A., LL.B., F.R.A.S., and G. H. BRYAN, M.A. 1s. 6d.

Trigonometry, The Tutorial. [*In preparation.*

Trigonometry, Synopsis of Elementary. *Interleaved.* 1s. 6d.

"An admirable little handbook."—*Lyceum.*

"For its purpose no better book could be recommended."—*Educational News.*

"Pithy definitions, numerous formulæ, **and terse explanatory** notes."—*Schoolmaster.*

"The facts could hardly be better given."—*Freeman's Journal.*

Sciences.

Analysis of a Simple Salt. With a Selection of Model Analyses. By WILLIAM BRIGGS, M.A., LL.B., F.C.S., and R. W. STEWART, D.Sc. Lond. Third Edition, with TABLES OF ANALYSIS (on linen). 2s. 6d.

"Likely to prove a useful and trustworthy assistance to those for whom it is especially intended."—*Nature.*

"Every help that can be given, short of oral instruction and demonstration, is here given; and not only will the private student find this a welcome aid, but the class-master will be glad of the help furnished by Messrs. Briggs and Stewart, whose names are a guarantee of accurate information."—*Education.*

"Its treatment of the subject in hand is very thorough, and the method is on sound lines."—*Schoolmaster.*

"The selection of model analyses is an excellent feature."—*Educational Times.*

Elementary Qualitative Analysis. By the same Authors. 1s. 6d.

Biology, Text-Book of. By H. G. WELLS, B.Sc. Lond., F.Z.S., F.C.P. With an INTRODUCTION by Prof. G. B. HOWES, F.L.S., F.Z.S.

    PART I., Vertebrates. *Second Edition.* 6s. 6d.
    PART II., Invertebrates and Plants. 6s. 6d.

"The *Text-Book of Biology* is a most useful addition to the series already issued, it is well arranged, and contains the matter necessary for an elementary course of vertebrate zoology in a concise and logical order."—*Journal of Education.*

"Mr. Wells' practical experience shows itself on every page; his descriptions are short, lucid, and to the point. We can confidently recommend it."—*Educational Times.*

"The numerous drawings, the well arranged tables, and the careful descriptions will be of the utmost value to the student."—*Schoolmaster.*

"Mr. Wells deals with everything he ought to deal with, and touches nothing that he ought not to touch. For the higher forms of Modern Side we commend this text-book without reserve; for the special student of biology we urge its use with enthusiasm."—*Educational Review.*

Chemistry, Synopsis of Non-Metallic. With an Appendix on Calculations. By WILLIAM BRIGGS, M.A., LL.B., F.C.S. *Interleaved.* 1s. 6d.

"The notes are very clear, and just the thing to assist in the revision of the subject."—*Literary Opinion.*

"Arranged in a very clear and handy form."—*Journal of Education.*

Heat and Light, Elementary Text-Book of. By R. W. STEWART, D.Sc. Lond. *Second Edition.* 3s. 6d.

"A student of ordinary ability who works carefully through this book need not fear the examination."—*The Schoolmaster.*

"It will be found an admirable text-book."—*Educational News.*

"A well-printed and well-illustrated book. It strikes us as a trustworthy guide."—*Practical Teacher.*

"A welcome addition to a useful series."—*School Guardian.*

Sciences—*continued.*

Magnetism and Electricity, Elementary **Text Book of:** Being an Abridgment of the *Text-Book of Magnetism and Electricity*, with 143 Diagrams and numerous Questions. By R. W. STEWART, D.Sc. Lond. 3s. 6d.

"Plain and intelligible. It is a capital example of what a good Text-book should be."—*Educational News.*

"Will prove to be particularly helpful to students in general."—*Science and Art.*

"We can heartily recommend it to all who need a text-book."—*Lyceum.*

"This is an admirable volume. A very good point is the number of worked-out examples."—*Teachers' Monthly.*

"Leaves little to be desired."—*Educational Times.*

"Another of his excellent text-books."—*Nature.*

THE TUTORIAL PHYSICS.

I. Sound, Text-Book of. By E. CATCHPOOL, B.Sc. Lond. 3s. 6d.

II. Heat, Text-Book of. With 81 Diagrams and numerous Calculations. By R. W. STEWART, D.Sc. Lond. *Second Edition.* 3s. 6d.

"**Clear,** concise, well arranged and well illustrated, and, as far as we have tested, accurate."—*Journal of Education.*

"Distinguished by accurate **scientific knowledge** and lucid explanations."—*Educational Times.*

"The principles of the subject are clearly set forth, and are exemplified by carefully chosen examples."—*Oxford Magazine.*

III. Light, Text-Book of (uniform with the *Text-Book of Heat*). With 111 Diagrams and numerous Calculations. By R. W. STEWART, D.Sc. Lond. *Second Edition.* 3s. 6d.

"**The diagrams** are neat and accurate, the printing excellent, and the arrangement of the matter clear and precise."—*Practical Teacher.*

"The volumes (*Light and Heat*) will be found well adapted for general use by those students who have already mastered the first principles of physics. The subjects are treated both mathematically and experimentally, and the most important theorems are illustrated by diagrams and figures."—*School Guardian.*

IV. Magnetism and Electricity, Text-Book of. With 159 Diagrams. By R. W. STEWART, D.Sc. Lond. *Second Edition.* 5s. 6d.

"Will be found suitable for general use as an introduction to the study of electrical science."—*Iron.*

"It is thoroughly well done."—*Schoolmaster.*

"The author has been very successful in making portions of the work not ordinarily regarded as elementary appear to be so by his simple exposition of them."—*Teachers' Monthly.*

Directories.

Matriculation Directory, with Full Answers to the Examination Papers. (*No. XVII. will be published during the fortnight following the Examination of January* 1895.) Nos. IV., VI., VII., IX., X., XI., XII., XIII., XIV., XV., and XVI. 1s. each, *net*.

Intermediate Arts Directory, with Full Answers to the Examination Papers (except in Special Subjects for the Year). (*No. VII. will be published during the fortnight following the Examination of July* 1895.) No. II. (1889) to No. VI. (1893), 2s. 6d. each, *net*.

Inter. Science and Prelim. Sci. Directory, **with Full Answers to the Examination Papers.** (*No. V. will be published during the fortnight following the Examination of July* 1895.) **No. I.** (1890) to No. IV. (1893). 2s. 6d. each, *net*.

B.A. Directory, **with Full Answers to the Examination Papers** (except in Special Subjects for the Year.) No. I., 1889; II., 1890; III., 1891. 2s. 6d. each, *net*. No. IV., 1893 (with Full Answers to the Papers in **Latin, Greek,** and Pure Mathematics). 2s. 6d. *net*. (*No. V. will be published in November* 1895.)

The University Correspondent

AND

UNIVERSITY CORRESPONDENCE COLLEGE MAGAZINE.

Issued every Saturday. Price 1d., by Post 1½d.; Half-yearly Subscription, 3s.; Yearly Subscription, 5s. 6d.

THE UNIVERSITY CORRESPONDENT has a wide circulation among Grammar and Middle Class Schools, and, as a weekly journal, offers an excellent medium for Advertisements of POSTS VACANT AND WANTED; no charge for these is made to Yearly Subscribers.

LEADING FEATURES OF "THE UNIVERSITY CORRESPONDENT."

1. *Fortnightly Prizes of One Guinea.*
2. *Frequent Vigilance Prizes (One to Three Guineas).*
3. *Special Prizes (One to Five Guineas).*
4. *Hints and Answers to Students reading for London University.*
5. *Answers to Correspondents on all University Matters.*
6. *Papers set at London Examinations.*
7. *Full Solutions to Matriculation Papers.*
8. *Pass Lists of London University Examinations.*
9. *Calendar of London University Events.*
10. *Latest University News.*
11. *Test Papers (with Answers) for London Matriculation.*
12. *Articles on Special Subjects for London University Examinations.*
13. *A Series of Articles on the Universities of the United Kingdom.*
14. *Ladies' Column.*
15. *Reviews of Current Educational Literature.*
16. *List of Educational Books published during the month.*

www.ingramcontent.com/pod-product-compliance
Lightning Source LLC
Chambersburg PA
CBHW030354170426
43202CB00010B/1376